Teaching
Barefoot in
Burma

Robert Edward Sterken Jr.

Robert Edward Sterken Jr.

Teaching Barefoot in Burma

Insights and Stories from a
Fulbright Year in Myanmar

Forward by Alison Johnson Sterken

Yangon, Myanmar

Published in 2016 by YSPS Publishing House: Yangon School of Political Science Press, No. 122 51st Street, Suite 300, Yangon, Myanmar. YSPS Publishing House License number: 01833.

ISBN-10: 0-692-77784-9.

ISBN-13: 978-0-692-77784-8.

Printed in the United States of America.

Cover photo credit: Alison Johnson Sterken.

This publication is not affiliated with the United States Fulbright Program, the United States Department of State, or the Institute of International Education. Nothing in this book represents the positions or opinions of the United States Department of State, the US Embassy in Myanmar.

*For Alison who made this journey with me, possible,
and a success. I am ever grateful, my love.*

and

For my Myanmar friends.

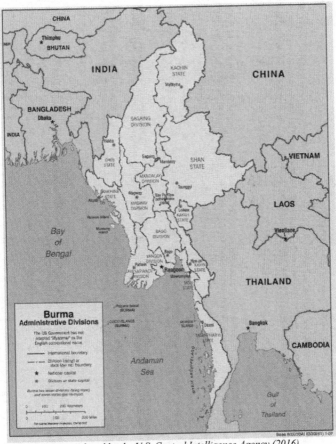

Map produced by the U.S. Central Intelligence Agency (2016).

"Sail Forth- Steer for the deep waters only. Reckless O soul, exploring. I with thee and thou with me. For we are bound where mariner has not yet dared go. And we will risk the ship, ourselves, and all." ~ Walt Whitman

◊

"Life is a dance. Mindfulness is witnessing that dance." ~ Amit Ray

◊

"The only way to make sense out of change is to plunge into it, move with it, and join the dance." ~ Alan Watts

Contents

◊

Forward

The author of this book, I often say, is like a silk suit. He looks great but he doesn't travel well. Though he is drawn to travel, longs to not only observe but to be totally immersed in other cultures, he is at heart and soul a home body, one who clings to hearth and family. This is one of many odd paradoxes of Dr. Robert E. Sterken Jr. He is truly an introvert who excels at public speaking. He is an award winning professor and teacher, beloved by his students, but he considers any organized socializing, any "event" outside of spending time with close friends and family, to be arduous and trying. For Bob, these social "events" are work.

In Texas, Bob loves the creature comforts of our home, from his morning Peets coffee dispersed piping hot and fresh from his Keurig, to his comfortable bed, clad in 500 thread count sheets, at night. In between, he enjoys our "Energy Star" certified, temperature moderating, air conditioning unit which efficiently and easily cools our home, his side-by-side stainless steel refrigerator which delivers filtered ice and water straight from the door, and his Bausch electric dishwasher that renders sparkling, sanitized glasses, plates, pots, and pans.

In Texas, he writes, works, and grades a ton of papers in his orderly home office, listening to Spotify play lists, while depending upon steady electricity, a high speed internet connection that reliably streams video and delivers a connection upon demand, for any number of devices simultaneously. He watches his home team, the Houston Astros, via our direct satellite.

Even more than the comforting routines of home, Bob values family. He was the dad who coached little league, helped with homework, drove carpool, played guitar and sang lullabies beside the bassinette, crib, toddler and big kid bed. He delights in home cooked meals, walking the dogs around our tree lined East Texas neighborhood, riding bikes with our now adult children, and running the recreation trails through Rose Rudman Park, adjacent to our subdivision. His favorite way to spend an evening is at home, with friends and family, drinking a nice glass of wine or a frosted mug of craft beer, and listening to music or catching a game. In October 2015, he left all of that behind and went to live in Myanmar for a year.

When we first arrived in Myanmar, the country was still considered to be a pariah state under the rule of the Union Solidarity and Development Party, an oppressive military junta (in power since 1962). We were required to go through an orientation with various members of the state department at the U.S. Embassy compound in Yangon. One of those officers was Ms. Lana Smith [name changed] who serves as the Regional Security Officer with the Diplomatic Security office. Lana is a federal law enforcement officer and her agency is charged with the protection of the U.S. Secretary of State. We were told to "always have a plan for non-violent crimes of opportunity," and to avoid being out at night. Though ex-pats are not issued driver licenses in Myanmar we were told not to take the buses as they are "filthy, poorly maintained, frequently break down, and are very dangerous; bus drivers drive like maniacs."

We were warned to be careful with taking taxis, to avoid taxis that were occupied by two people in the front seat, and not to share taxis with strangers. We were advised to check the cabs before getting in, and before negotiating the fare with the driver, as many are powered by natural gas tanks (in the back) and though some cab drivers make attempts to cover or camouflage the tanks, many are visible. Some have been known to explode on impact; trucks powered by natural gas have exploded spontaneously. In Myanmar, lane driving is optional and traffic laws are non-existent. Lastly, we were told to take special care when walking, as pedestrians do not have the right of way (as they do in the U.S.) and as the sidewalks (where they exist) were hazardous.

Most disturbing, we were told not to expect to have any personal privacy. We were to expect our phone calls, Facebook posts and private messages, and Twitter accounts to be monitored. Further, it would not be at all unusual for us to find ourselves being followed (by a member of the "special branch of military intelligence"). We were warned to be very careful with what we posted on Facebook, particularly avoiding anything derogatory about the government or any entity run by the government. We were not to post anything about the Buddha or to get a tattoo of the Buddha below the waist and we were never, ever, to display a photo of the Buddha, or take a photograph of any military staff or building owned by the military.

Because the results of the 2010 election were ultimately not recognized by the ruling party, there was considerable unrest following that election, and thus there was much uncertainty and a good amount of anxiety in the air regarding the upcoming post-election period. Because of this, Lana recommended carrying different SIM cards with us at all times and stated that texting might be the only way to communicate in the post-election period. As if preparing for a natural disaster we were warned to stock up on food, water, and money because we might find ourselves sheltering in place for a long period of time. We were to designate a meeting up plan, in case something happened and we were not together. We were to stay away from protests and political rallies. Like teenagers with a curfew, we were to insure that the embassy knew of our whereabouts at all times and to inform them if we were leaving the city of Yangon. This was our first introduction to the Yangon where Bob was to spend a year teaching.

Because Myanmar is a developing nation, for the expat, things often did not go according to our wishes. I have heard other expats describe life in Myanmar as "camping." Innumerable people have asked me if Bob is serving in the Peace Corps after learning the location of his Fulbright. The images that the Peace Corps brings to mind, one of primitive circumstances and constant sacrifice, were not so far from Bob's daily reality. Life in Myanmar is really rather similar to camping. The internet was intermittent as was the electricity. Power outages were almost a daily occurrence. We were fortunate that the building where the apartment was located had a large generator but we had to be present to activate the generator when the power failed.   So, with limited power, no one home to activate the generator, and AC restrictions, food in the refrigerator often spoiled before it could be cooked or eaten. Electric or gas powered clothes dryers did not exist, and clothes were whipped into submission to hasten drying by the hyperactive, low capacity washing machines, and then once hung to dry on the line, the humidity rendered a soured and stiffened board rather than a wearable garment.

Fresh fruits and vegetables, along with fish and chicken are available in the open air markets but with the lack of an FDA or equivalent, there are no assurances of safety.   There are no regulations insuring proper handling or refrigeration or cooking methods. On more than one occasion I recognized the same fish hanging in the late afternoon sun that I had greeted some 9 hours earlier.

The Myanmar people are skilled at many things but viniculture is not one of them.   Myanmar wine is unpalatable, and imported wine was difficult to find and was very expensive when it was available. Western plumbing and basic bathroom amenities are becoming more common, but were extremely expensive (New York prices). There was a shower in our Myanmar bathroom, but it offered only cold water. The mattress that came with our apartment was one of the best that could be found in Myanmar, but it was hard and unforgiving and we often awoke with sore backs, and even bruised hips.

Having been raised in Lubbock, Texas, I thought I was accustomed to harsh weather and weather extremes but my assumption was naïve. The heat in Myanmar, a country tucked in just above the equator, is insufferable and indescribable to one that has not experienced it firsthand. One often hears "it's not the heat, it is the humidly" in descriptions of Texas weather conditions but in Myanmar, it IS the heat and it IS the humidity. Near the equator, the sun's rays are coming in at a steep angle close to 90 degrees. This means that the sun's rays are concentrated. The heat per unit is higher at low latitudes which means the heat of the sun on our pale skin is insufferable.

For years, Bob has answered the call of wanderlust and during summer months has led students on sojourns to many countries in Europe, and many in Southeast Asia where his area of interest, religion and politics, has great bearing and a prominent presence. When he was awarded a Senior Fulbright to Myanmar, a Buddhist country on the brink of historic political change, where religion is intertwined with politics, there was no question that he would go, that he would answer this particular call, but it came at a price. Almost every single daily life necessity for peace, comfort, and self-fulfillment, from the most basic amenity, food, water, restful sleep, to the more esoteric, family, love, meaningful touch, was absent from his life. If suffering is distress, experiencing the unpleasant situations on a daily basis, moment to moment, hardship, separation from loved ones, then Bob surely suffered.

But as in Buddhist teachings, he has also recognized

the happiness, the irrepressible hopefulness, the courage, the joy and the loveliness of the Myanmar people. He witnessed the awakening of his students, as they realized what democracy could mean for their country. He taught political theory and the practical application of the principles of democracy to hundreds of students, and also Myanmar government officials and members of the Myanmar Parliament who will lead their country forward from five decades of brutality.

The suffering of his neighbors has given him perspective not available when living next door to other middle class Americans. While his shower may not have rendered warm water, the hose attached to the fiberglass tub did, and it was pure luxury when compared to the steel drum half filled with tepid water and a plastic bucket used to dump water over one's head, shared by every member of the extended family, in the lean to shack that bumps up against his apartment building. While his mattress was hard and uncomfortable, many of his neighbors slept on large pieces of suspended plywood or mats or on the ground. While life in Myanmar is less than optimal for the expat, it is ever forefront in the expat's mind that he can leave (I left and came back to the states to look after family in the U.S. numerous times). For our neighbors, the people who have no choice but to eat in the local markets, to bathe in the oil drum, and to live on a wages so far below the US poverty level that it does not even register on the scale, cannot.

In the time that Bob was in Myanmar he taught students at Myanmar Institute of Theology, Yangon School of Political Science, (which was underground during the years of the Junta government control), and Yangon University, (where the Political Science department was completely eliminated by the military). I was fortunate to observe him as he taught these classes. At the University of Texas at Tyler, Bob is known for his high energy, his unbridled enthusiasm for learning, his passion for his subject, his concern for the well-being of his students, particularly those without resources, (as he once was) and for his creative teaching techniques. His teaching style was largely unchanged by the limitations inherent in the classroom environment offered at the Myanmar institutions, no Wi-Fi, no air conditioning or even electric fans, often no electricity and typically he would be drenched with sweat before the class was halfway done.

In Texas, Bob is a habitual shoe wearer, donning his footwear from the time he begins his day until he goes to bed, even if he does not leave the house, but in Myanmar, shoes are not worn in the classroom. Teaching sans shoes may have been as much as a challenge as teaching sans air conditioning. In Myanmar, where there has been such a drought in the learning arena for so very long, he is an anomaly, an oddity so rare that the students were astounded, even taken aback by his mode of delivery, his enthusiastic and animated teaching style. They did not know what to think, but the point is, they did think. They listened, and absorbed, and took copious notes, and they learned and eventually they took part in the discussions. They came alive, moving from sitting quietly and obediently, to challenging one another and bringing forth new ideas of their own for discussion. Among their numbers were Muslims,

Buddhists, Christians, many former political prisoners, who spent years in the criminally inhumane Insein Prison, for standing up for human rights, and as previously mentioned, current and incoming members of the new democratic parliament.

Myanmar is on the cusp of major change, albeit it will not occur quickly enough for the country's fifty-four million citizens. The destruction, devastation, and demoralization that resulted from years of human rights violations and impoverishment took place over fifty-plus years and it will not be reconditioned overnight. It will take time and resources to rebuild the infrastructure of the country. But without leaders, without those well versed in the inner workings of democracy, it will not happen. When life was most difficult, when Bob despaired at what he had set aside to spend a year in Myanmar, I would remind him, "you are teaching the future leaders of this country, you are providing them with the tools that they will need to pull their people up out of poverty and to restore their civil and human rights."

Alison Johnson Sterken

Alison Johnson Sterken gives a speech on human rights in Yangon (2015).
Photo credit: Robert Sterken.

Preface

◊

I wrote this book during the Myanmar rainy season on the balcony of our seventh floor apartment overlooking the Hledan area of the city of Yangon. I was almost done with a journey of a lifetime. Almost two years earlier, it was also raining as I searched the front of the buildings on K Street in Washington, DC for the number 1400. Once I found the building and ducked inside, I told the guard that I had an appointment on the seventh floor in the offices of the United States Fulbright Scholar Program (he was unimpressed). After some checking, I was sent up and met by a receptionist who asked me to wait in the lobby. While seated, I wondered why I was actually there at all. I had applied for a Senior Fulbright Scholar grant nearly a year earlier and still had no answer. So while in Washington on other business, I decided to stop in the Fulbright offices, say hello, and just perhaps learn what was happening with my application. I did not then know and would not learn for many months that my application was on hold because of the Myanmar Ministry of Education.

Ms. Veronica Onorevole, the agent in charge of scholars appointed to Southeast Asia, greeted me kindly but formally and showed me to a large conference room. We chatted for what seemed like too long. Small talk is not enjoyable for me and most of what she was telling me was how difficult it is to win a Fulbright. I was sitting there feeling discouraged when after a while she slid a large

envelope across the table to me. I asked her what it
was and she smiled and said, "just open it." So I did.
The contents of that envelope changed my life. I had
been awarded a grant for a year of teaching and
research in Burma (the US State Department still
officially refers to the country as Burma). After
receiving words of congratulations from Veronica and
few other Fulbright staff, I walked out of the building
into the Washington, DC cold and rain just stunned. I
told no one of the news. I walked back to my hotel
thinking about how different the world already
seemed. I was going to live in Burma. I had never
even been to Burma. I would teach politics in a
university and conduct research on religion and
politics in a country that has been cut-off from the
rest of the world for the last sixty years. Two days
later, back at home in Texas I stopped my life partner,
Alison, as she was about to enter our laundry room
and handed her the envelope that Veronica had given
me in Washington. She screamed with joy and
delight, hugged me tightly, and immediately shared
the news with family and then on Facebook with the
world. Alison was gracious with the news even
though it meant lots of changes, struggle, and
sacrifice. I did not know then how much change or
struggle was coming or how significant a year in a
very foreign land would actually be. It is not
hyperbole to say that it was nothing short of life
changing.

In the pages of this little book, I will share not only
my story, and insights, but also what I personally
learned of the story of the beautiful people of
Myanmar. Many people ask me, "how has living in
Burma changed you?" This book attempts to answer

that seemingly simple question. In short, this is my Fulbright travel memoir. The act of writing allowed me to sort, process, and put into words my experiences and insights. Writing allowed me to better understand much that would have been left unexplored. Others have written Fulbright guidebooks and travel guides about Myanmar and the people. That is not the purpose of this book. If you are traveling to or seeking to learn about Myanmar you will learn about the land and people in these pages, from the perspective of a teacher and researcher – not a tourist or short-term travel writer. This is a story of seeking and learning. My story is centered and focused on the suffering and beauty of the dance of life. In a loose way this story also follows Siddhārtha Gautama's ancient path to the Bodhi tree. This is not a book about religion, but Buddhists will see the pattern. In my research, I learned from many Theravada Buddhist monks, mediated, and even spent time in several different Buddhist monasteries. My research focused on religion (Buddhism) and politics. It is not my goal, nor is it possible, to summarize the doctrines of Buddhism in these few pages. However, I do relate stories and lessons I learned from Buddhism and my experiences with Buddhist monks. As such, I touch on only those actions and Buddhist doctrines that I directly experienced. Interested readers will elsewhere find countless books about Buddhism and the lives of Theravada monks.

This story is about what it was like to be a Fulbright Scholar in a distant and unfamiliar land. I share my observations about Myanmar, my struggles with culture shock (and reverse culture shock), struggles in being in foreign land for so long, trials in teaching, research, and the many joys. Travelers to any land and certainly future Fulbright scholars may find this book helpful. I detail not only the process and the experience of teaching and conducting research in a land like no other, but I also touch on some of what to expect from working closely with the United States State Department and the US Embassies while abroad. Teaching and conducting research in Myanmar was a wild and remarkable experience.

I met many inspiring people in Southeast Asia. I met former political prisoners, many other scholars, United States State Department officials, many Buddhist monks, ambassadors from all over the world, many amazing Southeast Asian academics, and thousands of Myanmar and Thai college students. I even met and gave a presentation to Her Royal Highness Princess Maha Chakri Sirindhorn and the military cadets from the Thailand Chulachomklao Royal Military Academy. I enjoyed very fine celebrity chef prepared dinners with ambassadors. I ate lots of fried rice, Shan noodles, peanut butter sandwiches, and pasta alone in my apartment. I ate food I had not before considered edible and in settings most Americans would not dream of being – much less dining. Again, to say that my life has been greatly enriched is a significant understatement.

This is an informal and brief book. With a breezy read in mind and a healthy degree of guilt, I uncharacteristically did not include footnotes. My purpose here is to share my personal stories, lessons, and observations and not to create a scholarly tome about Myanmar. All I record here is as accurate as I could manage (some names have been changed at the request of those I've written about). Readers who are concerned about details or who simply want to know more will find a quick internet search quite revealing. I am grateful for and humbled by the experience and hope that sharing it here will bring some light to a land that is only just now opening to the outside world. I hope that my story will inspire you to journey outside your comfort zone and find your own Myanmar. I hope that my story helps you understand connection, bias, sacrifice, struggle, and mettā.

Her Royal Highness Princess Maha Chakri Sirindhorn presents a gift to Robert Sterken (2016). Photo credit: Royal Palace Thailand Media Services.

Chapter 1

A Fulbrighter in Myanmar: A Land Like No Other

◊

Unlike Any Land You Know

I was scared. Well, I was scared and worried. I was afraid of the unknown. I am after all, at heart, just a simple farm boy from rural route two, box five-three-four Alvin, Texas. I'm also one of the lucky global citizens who has, as an adult, widely traveled our global village. I had even traveled to Southeast Asia several times. But this was different. Travel for days, weeks, or even a couple of months is different from renting an apartment and finding a person to cut your hair. I couldn't back out, there had been media releases and billboards (no kidding, actual billboards) announcing my Fulbright award. Dr. Sterken was going to Burma. As a Fulbright scholar I was to teach and conduct research. Those activities came to fruition and I share some of that in this book, but the real story is the suffering and beauty – the dance of life – I found along the way. In Burma, I stepped way outside my ordinary and way beyond my comfort zone. There were many days when I wondered aloud to Alison about my ability to finish the journey.

As the date for our departure neared, I worried. Some nights I lay awake listening to the quiet breathing of my partner, looking at my dark, quiet, and comfortable bedroom wondering, if I might be crazy. The country in which I would be living was on the precipice of a major historic, political moment. Civil unrest, a military crackdown, and violent protests were entirely possible. There was even some question if the United States State Department would allow me to go. Months passed and I did not know if or when I would be traveling. I would be far away from family, friends, and the familiar. This was way beyond anything I'd ever done before. I was actually moving to a land like no other. What would it be like to live, research, and teach in the isolated land of pagodas, thanaka, heat, Thingyan, betel, longyis, Buddhists, monsoon rains, dengue fever, a military government, monks, nuns, and could I actually do it? What would happen to me? Would I be safe? Would the water make me sick? Could I run? Would I have a phone and regular internet access? What would I eat? What if I needed medical care? My mind raced on and on with wild, serious, and mundane questions. The struggles, challenges, adventures, people, and even the answers to the most mundane of questions brought insights, lessons, and gifts of a lifetime.

In 1898, Rudyard Kipling wrote: "This is Burma, and it is quite unlike any land you know about." It is still such in 2016 – although rapidly changing. Still, most of the people in Myanmar today live as they have for centuries. They lead simple lives directly tied to the land and to their daily existence. Even after having suffered under decades of harsh military rule, the people of Myanmar have a beautiful sparkle, obvious resilience, and a playfulness that shines in their everyday lives. Myanmar women often walk hand-in-hand with their female friends. Both men and women wear the longyi – a long straight skirt wrapped around and tied at the waist. Everyone wears sandals. Closed toe shoes are rare. Pagodas (a place of worship) are everywhere. It is common to see two men walking together in the streets of Yangon or Mandalay with arms draped over each another's shoulders, or sitting together in a tea shop resting a hand on the other's knee. Myanmar men show affection to one another in ways that American men are deprived.

The people hold annual spirit-prayer festivals and the political protests of passionate students are legendary. It is these contrasts, the rich diversity, and the ancient religious traditions that make Myanmar a remarkable and fascinating land. It is in this land and among these people that I lived, studied, taught, and learned. I interviewed monks and drank tea with strangers. I visited with taxi drivers and saw ancient pagodas and ate the local food and drank local beer. I woke to the sound of chanting monks and visited with my neighbors and interviewed my students.

I plunged deeply into life in Myanmar. I experienced two earthquakes, and moved, as best I could manage, with the pace and rhythm of the local life. I participated in the dance. I came to see the swirling and confusing nature of it all, as just that – a dance of human existence. The honking horns in the stop-and-go traffic, the clapping of flip-flops as people walked, the raindrops on umbrellas, the morning slurping of fish soup, and the quiet resting of old men in curved teak chairs all made up a beautiful swirling and often dizzying dance. Even the names of people and places illustrate the confusing and ever-changing dance of life in Burma.

Names, Myanmar or Burma?

Names in Myanmar – both individual personal names and the names of cities, parks, rivers, mountains, ethnic peoples, and even the name of the country itself – are complex. Almost all of the names I use in this book are the person's real and actual names. Some names have been changed to hide the person's identity. Many of the people I write about in these pages can be found with a quick internet search. The media is Myanmar in 2016 is beginning to have the freedom to publish freely, but many individuals (many monks) asked me not to use their names or their photos. I have respected those wishes.

While family ties are strong in Myanmar, each individual has his or her own personal name, which is often very different from everyone else in the family. For example, during the time that my wife, Alison, and I lived in Yangon, we shared our apartment with Hjar Hjar Binks (the H is silent). Hjar Hjar is a tiny Pacific house gecko, an anthropomorphized Buddhist lizard, who decided to reside on the balcony of our seventh floor apartment. Hjar Hjar Binks' name is typical in Myanmar, as almost all names in Myanmar are personal. Personal both in the sense that one night I just started calling him after the Star Wars character (he seemed fine with it), and also personal in that almost all names in Myanmar are person specific. There are no surnames in the Myanmar culture, even within the same nuclear family. Also, in Myanmar, geckos like Hjar Hjar are believed to be a good omen and I needed all the good omens I could get. Hjar Hjar, is nocturnal, and slept during the days and foraged for insects at night on our balcony. In the end, Hjar Hjar came to remind me of an important life principle.

Burma or Myanmar?

The name of the country is even more complex. Is it Burma or Myanmar? In one of my visits to Thailand, a senior United States State Department official, who was about to introduce me to a Thai audience, whispered, "I know I should know this, but is it Burma or Myanmar?" I laughed. It not something one should be embarrassed about, as the answer depends on who you ask. The United States State Department still calls the country Burma, for political reasons. What to call the country is like many things in Myanmar, about politics. For centuries the name of the people (Burman) was the name of the country – Burma. But that changed in 1988.

On the 8th day of August in 1988 the people of Burma had had enough. Their economy was in shambles and, more urgently, the price of fuel oil was suddenly unaffordable. From 1962 until 1988, the country was ruled by its brutal military led by General Ne Win. The August 8th 1988 protests (now called the 88 uprising) started with students of Yangon University and quickly spread throughout the country. Hundreds of thousands of monks, students, and people from all walks of life demonstrated against the military government. In my time in Myanmar, I came to observe the impact of those protests and to know many people whose lives had been altered by this 88 uprising (more on this later).

The 88 uprising ended on the eighteenth of September, following a military coup. The new military leaders (who were just as brutal as their predecessors) decided to rename – almost everything – including the country. In 1989 the military decreed that the country would be called the Union of Myanmar. The word "Myanmar" dates back to the 12th century and carries a literal meaning of "a strong and fast people." This decree (new law) not only affected the name of the country by also people (ethnicities) and many landmarks and cities within the country. The city of Rangoon was renamed Yangon. Streets that the British had named Windermere Court, Fraser Street, and Montgomery Road, for example, were given new names. The Irrawaddy River was renamed the Ayeyawady. The Karen State, which is on the border with Thailand, became Kayin State. City parks, major lakes, and many streets were renamed. Objections to all of these name changes came almost immediately and from all across the world. Because of the nature of the brutal military regime the name changes were viewed with skepticism by world leaders.

The new names came to be associated with and to symbolize the military regime that had so violently and brazenly ignored the will of the 88 protests. The exact number of deaths is not known, but has been estimated to be around 3,000 people, mostly students. Many countries around the world duly noted the name changes and went on with business as usual. This, however, was not the case for the Americans or the

British. The United States, expressing solidarity with the Burmese people and opposing the military, refused to acknowledge the name changes and still does in 2016. The people in the country routinely call their country Myanmar. The Americans and the British use Burma. I use both in this book.

An Urgent Departure/Arrival

The United States Embassy officials were quite demanding about the time frame during which my wife, Alison, and I were to arrive in Burma. They demanded that we arrive before October 15, or, they emphatically wrote, we would not be going at all. The US Embassy in Yangon and the entire country was in the throes of an historic and potentially dangerous election. The Embassy wanted us to be settled well before the November 8th general election date. Because we could not book air tickets until we had our visas in hand, we had to wait until the last minute and thus paid a premium for our air tickets with a United States owned airline. Federal law (Fly America Act) requires all Fulbright Scholars, and others on US government business, to travel on only American air carriers. The urgency added to the anxiety of the entire undertaking.

We landed at Yangon International airport very late at night and were simply exhausted after twenty-eight hours of travel on three flights and two layovers. Fifty years of isolation make arrival in Burma like stepping back in time. The architecture and colors of the airport terminal (since remodeled) were from a long gone era. The terminal and airport were originally built on what was a World War II British RAF airfield. It had been updated since WWII, but obviously not in decades. In our traveler's fog the ubiquitous lime-green walls were shocking. We waited anxiously in the "foreigner" line for an immigration officer.

The Immigration form asked if I was carrying $10,000 or more in US dollars. Technically speaking, I wasn't. In reality, Alison and I were carry more crisp $100 bills that I had ever seen before. Being from a country where we hardly ever use actual cash or coins, it was a strange thing to walk up to the teller at my bank in Tyler, Texas and ask for $12,000 in crisp one-hundred dollar bills. I wasn't doing anything illegal, but I was nervous and the teller knew it. In Myanmar, vendors will absolutely not accept a bent or marked US bill. No exceptions. The bills must be absolutely pristine. I know that to American readers this sounds odd. One monk that Alison and I later interviewed brought out an old $100-dollar bill and asked us if we would exchange it for a new bill. The bill looked fine, just old. No one in Myanmar would take it. Alison took it back to the United States and happily released it back into circulation.

Making Myanmar Home

Alison and I were taken to an expensive "Western" hotel that the US Embassy had arranged for us. While recovering from jet lag we started exploring our new city and meeting with university faculty and administrators. I was scheduled to start teaching in less than two weeks. After about six days of hotel living we were very ready to find our own place. Searching for an apartment in Yangon was a wild experience. In 2015, everyone told us that finding an apartment in Yangon would be a strange and very expensive nightmare. While we did find apartment hunting in Yangon to be strange – it was not as strange as many of the travel blogs and the media portrayed it to be. Maybe this had been so a few years earlier, but again, things are rapidly changing in Yangon and across the country.

One of the odd things about the 2015 Myanmar rental market was that the renter was expected to pay the entire twelve months of rent at once – up front. Not only all at once, but also in pristine $100 USD bills. Thus, many people, like Alison and me, arrived in Myanmar with a lot of cash. It took us about a week to find a suitable (meaning tolerable) apartment. We used three different agents to help us with the search. Riding around with the agents in hot taxis and deep into neighborhoods and into different parts of the city was both eye-opening and a bit nerve-wracking. Other expats were bidding on the same apartment units. In our apartment search, we visited with several weary American expats who were ready to be back in the United States. We walked past entire families as we checked out the "upstairs apartments." We saw many overpriced places that had little or no kitchen or western plumbing fixtures. Many of the apartments were just far too large for two people. Lighting was odd, the ceilings were frequently lined with bare florescent lights or alternately, with oversized neon lights in raised ceilings. Many units were devoid of windows and thus were dark and depressing. After about three or four days of searching we finally found a place that was within our budget and that would make an adequate home. The apartment looked far different from the typical American flat – but Alison made it a home. We bought some local art for the walls, some nice teak furniture, and a few rugs in the markets. We paid the agent her fee (half a month's rent) and gave the landlord rent for the first six months – in those crisp one-hundred dollar bills. We were fortunate; most renters must pay for the entire year in advance.

We lived just off of Insein Road, just across from the Yangon University buildings that house the History and International Relations Departments where I would later teach. The three of us, including Hjar Hjar, shared the apartment in the area of Hledan in the Kamayut township. The kitchen and balcony afforded us a clear view of the Judson Church tower on the campus of Yangon University which is along the southwestern bank of the beautiful Inya Lake. Inya Lake is an artificial reservoir created by the British in 1882, who called it Lake Victoria. Judson Church, on the main campus of Yangon University, is a Baptist church named after Adoniram Judson, a 19th-century American missionary. Today, as a direct result of Judson's work, about eight percent of Myanmar's population are Christian and most of those are Baptist.

Hjar Hjar Binks liked our kitchen and, on occasion, would be seen looking for water, and also, I assume, tiny bits of things lizards like to eat. Our housekeeper, Htuk Htuk Aung, was very efficient but she only came one day a week – so Hjar Hjar did not go hungry. In the evenings, when my beautiful life partner was not in Yangon, Hjar Hjar and I would sit on the balcony watching the life of the city below.

The area around our apartment was densely populated and held people from all walks of life. They lived in ways and in places that are difficult to describe. Unlike most people in Myanmar, Hjar Hjar was fluent in English and also well read, so we shared many delightful evenings together on the balcony (Alison and I made similar use of the balcony).

Traffic and Cycling

Getting around in 2016 Myanmar was an unhealthy nightmare. Traffic in Yangon was unbelievably congested and slow. For a person who hates the car culture this was a real struggle. Yangon is Myanmar's commercial capital, and it now rivals neighboring Bangkok and Jakarta for the worst traffic in Southeast Asia. Several factors have come together to make Yangon a traffic nightmare. First, Yangon's roads and highways are narrow, in bad shape, and simply cannot handle all of the demand. Many roads have not been maintained in decades. Second, when Myanmar began to open up in 2011, one of the first policy changes was to allow for the import of automobiles. Prior to this opening, the automobile market had been monopolized by just a handful of businesspeople with close links to the military. The policy change caused car prices, which had been for years were exceptionally and artificially inflated, to plummet. As a result, cars flooded the streets of Myanmar.

In August 2011 there were just 214,000 cars in Yangon, a city of 5.2 million people. When we arrived in Yangon in October 2015, there were more than 500,000 vehicles overcrowding the city's streets. Foreigners were not allowed to own cars (but some did anyway), most Myanmar people cannot afford to purchase them, there was no public transportation system, and motor scooters were not allowed in Yangon, so those who do not own cars had to use taxis or ride the horribly hot and unsafe privately owned buses. In 2016, there were over 100,000 taxis in Yangon (and many had a Buddha mounted on the dashboard). In comparison, New York City, home to 8 million people, but has fewer than 14,000 taxis.

Cycling

To avoid the sweaty and uncomfortable hours in Yangon's taxis, I bought a bicycle. I reasoned, that as the traffic moved agonizingly slow, I could easily and safely manage to get around and save a ton of time and frustration. My reasoning failed to include three important factors. First, with so many cars on the streets, taxi drivers often break the rules of the road to try to get to their destination just a bit faster. Second, the traffic lights are set at unusually long intervals, and third, lane-driving (driving in a specific lane) is only an option on the Yangon streets – not a requirement. There are bumper stickers and billboards that read, "lane driving is safe driving."

For months, I rode hundreds of miles around the city without incident. Well, I did have two incidents with betel nut. Many Myanmar men chew betel nuts, which are potent parcels of areca nuts and tobacco wrapped in a lime-coated betel leaf. The betel quids – or "nuts" as they are often called – are commonly used by taxi drivers as a stimulant to stay alert while driving. The issue for a cyclist is that taxi drivers often spit huge amounts of unsightly red saliva into the street. I was hit not once but twice. Alison was also hit once with betel spit (on her foot) while walking back from the market. I believe that the pace at which I cycled and Alison walked had something to do with the betel accidents. We moved considerably faster than the typical Myanmar citizen. In fact, I had to learn to slow down when walking Yangon's sidewalks. One night I met a German cyclist who told me he had given up riding after a pedestrian had stepped out in front of him, with the accident putting them both in the hospital. The pedestrian he had collided with was knocked unconscious for a time. Medical care in Myanmar is dismal. Anyone who can afford to do so flies to Bangkok for even the most routine of treatments.

One night on my way back from class, I was zipping down Pyay Road on my bike next to Inya Lake with the flow of the Corolla taxis (I have a GoPro video of a similar ride). The blinking light on my helmet was flashing and I was being cautious when the strain of a long day of congested journeys pushed an exhausted and irritable taxi driver to lose patience and suddenly pull out from a side road clipping the back tire of my Trek bicycle. Backpack, water bottle, and all, I flew over the handlebars to my left, catching my right thigh on the left handlebar, bending the bar, and then landing on the back of my left shoulder in the street. My helmet saved my head or I might not be writing this. I got up and assured the frightened and clearly distressed taxi driver that I was okay and that all was forgiven. I walked my bike the last mile back to the apartment. I was banged up, but thankfully had no broken bones. I followed my German friend's precedent and did not ride in Yangon traffic again.

Security Briefing

A few days after our arrival, Alison and I stopped by the US Embassy for our "security briefing." It was an odd experience. The woman (a US government police officer) who gave our briefing was from Georgia and had only recently arrived in Myanmar. In a dry-matter-of-fact kind of way, she read off a checklist of things that Alison and I should and should not do. We should avoid the ferry boats (they capsize from being overloaded). We should not post things to Facebook about the government (we could end up in prison). We should not post things about Buddha on Facebook or other media (we could end up in prison). She informed us that we would be closely watched and followed by government officials (if that happened they were excellent at never letting it be known).

Yes, Taxi Adventures

Chief on her security list was that we must stay out of taxis that had been converted from gasoline to natural gas. Many of Yangon's taxis (hundreds of thousands of white, old, and dirty Toyota Corolla wagons – most without air conditioning – brought in from South Korea and Japan) run on compressed natural gas. We were told that when hit from behind they explode. Alarming as that sounded however, it proved next to impossible to follow that warning. The taxis are not marked as running on natural gas and it is often hard to see if the taxi has a natural gas tank. I soon gave up even attempting to find out. Also, Yangon's taxis never have seat belts. It's as if seat belts were never installed.

Another reason it was an adventure to hail a Yangon taxi was that the drivers knew very little English, but would act as if they understood. Also, they often did not know how to read a map, and did not have any clue of the location of the intended destination, even after saying, "yes, I know." In Myanmar, many people will not give direct answers. Very often people say, "yes," even when they do not really mean it. People rarely say no. In fact, I have had people say, "yes" while shaking their head no, which is really confusing. Taxi drivers are also very reluctant to say no to foreigners. This is a real problem when negotiating with a taxi driver about a destination. I had a friend write out the addresses of places I frequently visit in Myanmar/Burmese. Like a lost kindergartner trying to get home, I simply handed the address to the driver. Most of the time they nodded and said yes and away we went. But it was not uncommon for the driver to start asking other drivers or pedestrians along the way for directions, or phone friends for help. I would follow along on GPS on my phone or iPad and would sometimes see that we were not going toward my destination. I did not have but one or two drivers who were able to read and understand GPS maps.

For the first month or so we were in Yangon, I would open Google maps on my iPad and show the driver the route and destination. The driver would, of course, say, "yes!" and then once we were on the road he would call a friend for help. One night Alison and I ended up so far from the restaurant we were planning to visit that we just found another restaurant in the part of the city the taxi driver had ended up taking us. It was always an adventure to hail a taxi!

Unlike other cities in the world, taxis in Yangon are not metered, which means there is no meter to calculate the fare. Therefore, one must bargain with the taxi driver for every trip. The foreigner almost always gets the higher "foreigner's price." When hailing a taxi with my Myanmar friends, they would always ask me to stand off a little way from the group, so that it would not look like the tall American was part of the deal. Alone, I always paid too much. With the asking price between $1.50 and $5 USD who could really complain. I certainly did not.

Our security briefing officer also told us to avoid using the Yangon buses. She said that Yangon's local buses were unsafe. I took a few buses and observed many. I suspect that actual injuries are few in number, but, the buses are in horrible condition. They are privately owned and operated without any government oversight. Imagine how much maintenance an owner might put into his or her buses without any oversight or government inspection. I will just tell you – very little, to none. The City of Yangon planned to begin a municipal bus service in 2017.

Grass Roots People

Yangon has a circular railway that rings the entire city. The railway is a relic of the 1960s, but many people still rely on it for daily transport, even though it is not at all efficient. I do, however, recommend, if you are ever in Yangon, a full afternoon ride on the decades-old, slow-moving train. From its windows you will see into the past. One of my Myanmar traveling companions described the people seen from the train as "the grass roots people." From the slow moving train, I saw everyday life. Mothers with babies strapped to their backs worked to prepare meals. Children with bare feet played ball in the dusty roads. Old men sat in chairs or lay in hammocks smoking cigars and watching the people on the train. Nuns under umbrellas made their way to schools. Yes, the people I saw and met are extremely poor by American standards, and I do not want to romanticize their lives, but I saw beautiful life – even joy – in the midst of what is hard. From my place of privilege, it was too easy to flinch and to pity, but I saw much laughter and many people were quick to smile at me. Somehow through all the poverty, government repression, heat, disease, and many other hardships, the people of Myanmar consistently exhibited a sense of humor mixed with a healthy dose of humility and compassion.

In 2016, democracy is taking hold in Myanmar. Taxis choke the streets of Yangon (and hit cyclists). Mobil phones are becoming ubiquitous. Bogyoke Market bustles with business (and child labor). Many children are walked to schools every morning (many do not have that opportunity). Construction cranes dominate the skylines of Yangon, Mandalay, and Nay Pyi Taw. The ports, airports, and border crossings are booming with trade. But too many people are still mired in severe poverty.

In 2016, the majority of Burmese citizens subsist on an average annual income of less than $200 USD. In June 2016, Myanmar's newly elected President U Htin Kyaw promised to increase spending on education, health, and social welfare and to focus on poverty alleviation and infrastructural development. The country is also struggling with religion and intolerance. Myanmar is at a unique crossroads in its history. What values will guide their next steps? Buddhism? Consumerism? Sustainable development? Islam? Secularism? Perhaps the people of Myanmar will find the middle way.

The Gig of a Lifetime

The Myanmar people are known for their teak (also jade and rubies). Myanmar's teak forests account for most the world's naturally occurring teak. Out of this beautiful and durable wood they make, among many other things, a special chair that is shaped sort of like a hammock. The students at my first teaching assignment, at the Myanmar Institute of Theology, gave me one of these beautiful chairs as a parting gift. Sitting in my comfortable teak chair on my balcony with Hjar Hjar on the wall beside me, I began writing this book.

I went to Myanmar seeking experiences, to teach, and in the pursuit of knowledge. I had defined specific plans and goals for my time. I am happy to say that I accomplished some of those plans and goals, Myanmar altered some of them, but I found something else in the process. At orientation in Washington, a Fulbright alum told me that the Fulbright was, "the gig of a lifetime." At the same orientation a Fulbright program administrator had a more worrisome story. In a bid to help us understand the isolation and need to take good care of ourselves, she told us about a scholar a few years earlier who checked in at the mid-year Fulbright conference emaciated and in such poor health that she had to be flown back to the US for medical care. Laying on the new, but uncomfortable, mattress in our Yangon apartment, I thought, this won't be so hard. But I suspected I might be wrong.

Robert Sterken visits with two former political prisoners, center Saffron monk and the other now a political scientist (2016). Photo credit: Alison Johnson Sterken.

Chapter 2

Culture Shock: Coffee, Being Tall, Foreign, and Looking Deeply

◊

Rice Fields

I grew up outside of a small town on the Texas Gulf Coast, in the middle of rice fields. Literally, the house I grew up in was surrounded by rice fields. From my bedroom window, I could see rice growing all the way to the horizon. A common bumper sticker on local pickup trucks read, "Have a rice day." Unlike in Myanmar, the rice fields in south Texas are extremely large, they routinely fly on the seed and tend to the crop from the air (for a long time I wanted to be a crop dust pilot). The rice fields around my childhood home were irrigated with water from a network of canals that brought millions of gallons of water from the Brazos River. When they flooded the fields (rice typically grows in water) it looked sort of like we lived on a lake. South Texas weather is not unlike Burma's – both are very humid and perfect for rice growing. The farming area where I grew up supplies American markets with rice by railroad, and Asian markets from ports in Houston and Galveston. In high school, I was a member of the Future Farmers of

America and for several years won prizes in judging rice. To judge rice, I studied rice, its history and origins. Yes, believe it or not, I could identity type, name, and explain the histories many different varieties of rice, from long and short grains to aromatic rice to the basmati rice that originates from Myanmar and Southeast Asia. Studying rice sparked an early interest in Asia, and a desire to travel the planet. As a sixteen-year-old, I learned that Burma had long been considered the world's "rice bowl." Myanmar's ancient history is inseparable from rice. Rice is the main food of the people of Myanmar, and is often served with meat or fish, soup, salad and vegetables. A favorite Myanmar breakfast dish is Mohinga, rice noodles served with fish soup. Fish soup for breakfast was a bit of shock.

From the beginning of the 20th century into the 1940s, Burma was the world's top rice producer. Until the 1960s, the decade before I started studying rice, Burma's rice farmers supplied the world with almost two million tons of rice each year – well more than any other country in the world (it is a country about the size of Texas). In the 1960s and 1970s, the military dictatorship destroyed rice production and in the process made Burma Southeast Asia's poorest nation. As a young person, my travel was limited to what I read in books and magazines. I saw Burma in the pages of my father's National Geographic magazine collection. I would hide from farm work to read about the people in faraway lands. Books allowed me to see the rice fields of Burma. I vowed that someday I would see those rice fields. In 2016, I not only saw them, but I also taught the children of Myanmar's rice farmers and had tea with some of those farmers at the edge of their rice fields. They were shocked that the Saya (professor) knew something of rice farming. Today, Myanmar's rice production is once again poised to regain some of its former glory. Myanmar's farmers are no longer solely focused on rice, farmers in the northern regions of the country are also growing wonderful coffee.

Make Your Coffee Slowly

In the months between learning I had been awarded a Fulbright and the departure date, I read every article and book I could find on the country and culture. I wanted to be prepared. I knew that living long-term in a new culture would be both a great gift and a substantial challenge (particularly one that had long been isolated and was seriously underdeveloped). I even began to plan how I might adapt. In my normal daily routine in the United States, I start each day with coffee. Just like many Americans, coffee is an important part of my morning routine. I enjoy the daily savoring of a simple cup of coffee. Once, while having a cup of coffee in the Kachin State (a state in the northern part of Myanmar that borders China and India) my host said, "I try to avoid all American luxuries, but there are two such luxuries that I cannot live without, those are hot showers and brewed coffee." During my daily coffee routine, it is my practice to follow Thich Nhat Hanh's advice. He said, "Drink your tea slowly and reverently, as if it is the axis on which the world earth revolves – slowly, evenly, without rushing toward the future." To continue this practice, I decided to purchase a Keurig brewer for my Yangon apartment.

Somewhere in Yangon, there are fifty Peets Keurig-cups (individual coffee pods). I expect those to be the only Keurig-cups in the entire country of Myanmar, since they are not sold there. They are unused and will, I expect, always remain so. The Keurig brewer I bought and carefully packed across the globe was instantly fried upon plugging it into the Yangon electrical system. So somewhere in the garbage dump of that vast city sits a very out-of-place broken white Keurig coffee maker. With the loss of Keurig brewer, my morning coffee routine changed. In the United States, I typically pour creamer into my favorite Peets cup and pop it into the microwave for exactly 42 seconds – so that the creamer and cup are both warm for the coffee. While the seconds ticked off, I routinely pull out a Peets Major Dickson K-cup and place it in the brewer so that it is ready for the warm creamer (sometimes I make Alison's coffee during that 42 seconds). The total coffee brewing time in the US takes less than two minutes. The coffee is good. The mess is minimal, even if the brewing method is environmentally unsustainable. I was forced to adapt in Myanmar.

Coffee in Myanmar is serious business. In June 2016, serious coffee artists gathered from the all over Southeast Asia to take part in the Myanmar Latte Art Competition. Audiences watched enthralled as baristas swiftly sculpted foam images in steamed milk and coffee. Myanmar produces about 7,000 tons of coffee beans a year. The United States Agency for International Development has been training Myanmar growers to produce a high-end specialty coffee (Arabica beans). The Arabica beans are normally double the price of a lower grade coffee.

There are no Caffè Nero or Starbucks shops in Myanmar yet, but foreign coffee shop chains have already started to discover Myanmar consumers. Australia's Gloria Jean's Coffees opened its first outlet in March 2016. Thai chains True Coffee, Black Canyon, and Chao Doi also opened shops in Yangon in 2016.

My Myanmar coffee routine was far different from my daily Texas routine. In Yangon, I ground Myanmar Arabica beans bought in a local market. I walked to the market every other day for groceries. The refrigerator in my apartment was very small and the electric power very frequently went out – foods do not last very long in the tropical heat. One Fulbright scholar told me that he placed an ice cube on the top rack of his freezer as a test. If the cube was gone when he returned, he knew that the power had been off long enough for the food in the fridge to spoil. After grinding the Myanmar grown Arabica beans, I then ran drinking water (tap water in Yangon is like Tyler water – you should not drink it) into the kettle. While waiting for the water to boil, I placed seven scoops of freshly ground coffee into a French press carafe. Once the water boiled, I let it cool for two minutes (it needs to be less than 212 for optimal brewing), and then poured it into the carafe soaking all of the coffee – but only filling it halfway. Then I waited for a couple of minutes before filling the carafe completely. I then let the coffee brew for three more minutes. I set a timer – as I was ready for coffee! Then I carefully put the lid on the carafe and plunged the press slowly and methodically to the bottom – this was a pleasure to do. While waiting another few minutes for the sediment to settle, and I admire the beauty of it all. The coffee is wonderful. Bold. The pace and ritual of it all is quite unique. The French press brewing became an enjoyable part of my morning routine. Back in the States, I continue my new coffee practice – slowly, evenly, and reverently, as if it is the axis on which the world revolves – without rushing toward the future.

Culture Shock!

By the end of my Fulbright year, I felt at ease in the Myanmar culture, but it took me several months to adjust completely to the culture shock. Having traveled widely and recently in Vietnam and Cambodia, the first few weeks in Myanmar were enjoyable and even easy (part of that was due to Alison's efforts to make our apartment a home). Every new experience: from apartment hunting, seeing new sights, trying new foods, meeting Myanmar faculty, to trying on a longyi was exciting, but, yes, still also taxing and stressful. After about a month or so, I noticed a sense of anxiety, even nervousness, and a feeling of alienation that crept into my days and nights. I awoke in the small hours of the night wondering – again – if I might be crazy. Sometimes I was unable to catch my breath. My first months of living in Myanmar exposed me to a dramatically new environment, culture, and very often left me feeling somewhat disoriented. I knew I was experiencing culture shock and that I needed to allow myself the time to acclimate and accept my new environment. But it was still challenging.

In year before the Fulbright, I took a small group of students to Cambodia and one of the students had been deeply shocked by the new culture and environment. Claiming to be ill, he refused to come out of his room. When I explained that culture shock was normal, he told me that he had traveled the world and so he refused to face the reality of culture shock. The result was that for him the trip was a great disappointment. For that student, the only solution was to go back to the US, which he tried to do after only a few days of a four-week trip. I believe that his refusal to face his culture shock made it impossible to overcome, and his negative thinking was a vicious cycle that quickly pulled him down.

The shock of the Myanmar culture hit me in waves. After about a month, life started to feel really odd. Some days I absolutely loved the country, people, and my new teaching post. Other days I relayed my feelings to Alison and emailed my negative feelings back to my colleagues and family in Texas. One night after class, I told one of my Myanmar colleagues that I felt like a bull in a China shop (a big, awkward person in a small room full of fragile things). I felt awkward, clumsy, and like I never quite knew what to say or how to act. Some nights I slept well, and other nights I awoke short of breath. I missed my home life, friends, and family. The language barrier became a real frustration, rather than a part of the adventure. I longed for a full conversation in English. Strangers I encountered who spoke in complete English sentences were at times the highlight of the day. I searched the grocery stores for familiar foods (I did not find many). I was frustrated with the traffic and how difficult it was to get anywhere. I was awkward, homesick, and too tall. I needed time to process all that I was experiencing. There were so many challenges throughout each day: dressing differently, teaching in a new environment with different expectations (and without my shoes), meeting new colleagues, observing and processing cultural differences, analyzing the meaning of what the Myanmar people were actually saying, and even watching my head as I walked to the market.

Being Tall

In the London tube, people are ever reminded to "mind the gap." Expats in Myanmar should be similarly reminded to "mind their heads." I constantly needed to watch my head. Signs across the sidewalks were almost always set at about six feet above the ground, I am six-foot-two. The average height of the people of Myanmar is almost a foot shorter. Gardeners regularly trim branches overhanging sideways to about six feet or less. The many vendors that line the streets and sidewalks of Yangon and Mandalay have carts loaded with foods and other goods. Each night, just after sunset many Myanmar people eat from street vendors. Charcoal fires are used to cook strange meats, whole fish, and cakes. Fried vegetables abound. There were many foods I could not imagine eating. To protect the food and cooking from the rains, each of those carts had either a mounted umbrella or a tin or plastic roof built on pipe. Often the edges of those roofs and umbrellas were ragged and are at about eye level for a tall American. After traveling in Vietnam, Cambodia, and Thailand, I was prepared to be "the strange, tall, very white guy." But Myanmar was different. Everywhere I went I felt like a giant. One afternoon, Alison and I were walking to the market when an excited and

laughing young many bounded away from the group
he was with, to walk shoulder-to-shoulder with me.
He wanted to compare his height to mine. Laughing
and pointing, he shouted to his friends that the top of
his head came to my shoulder. Many of the buildings
at Yangon University and in downtown Yangon were
built by the British well before World War II. In those
days (that ended in the 1940s), they did not build
ceilings and doorways to accommodate tall people. I
bumped my head more than a few times on food
carts, ran into multiple street vendor umbrellas, and
was hit by too many people carrying umbrellas to
count. Along with my very fair skin (that burns easily
in the tropical sun and refuses to tan) my height and
gray hair left me unable to blend in with the people of
Myanmar.

Poverty Shock

In Yangon it is not uncommon to see monks with
expensive robes, elaborate handbags, matching
umbrellas, and iPhones. I have seen monks being
driven in the latest model Lexus SUVs. Just like in
the United States and elsewhere around the world,
there are those members of the religious community
who greatly profit personally from their association
with the powers of religion. Conversely, I visited with
many monks who are doing remarkably good work.
One afternoon, three students and a fellow faculty
member took to me a monastic school about an hour
north of Yangon. The five of us all stuffed ourselves
into a small Toyota Corolla taxi and talked as we
bounced over rain soaked, very rough gravel, and
muddy roads. We arrived at the monastery at about
one in the afternoon and were greeted at the gate by a

very old monk with no teeth. He was dressed in shabby robes that were not tied well. He looked more like a homeless monk than member of a large monastic community. The old monk told our driver where to find the head monk. Following his directions our taxi driver drove around a few buildings and into a small courtyard. It was raining, so we quickly hurried inside the head monk's building.

It was very dark inside and the smell of poverty was overpowering. As my eyes adjusted to the dark, I saw that we were surrounded by sleeping novice monks. Sleeping on plywood shelves at various levels were about fifty or sixty boys in saffron robes. Some looked up at us with mild curiosity, most did not wake or stir. Removing our sandals at the foot of the stairs, we were shown upstairs to the head monk's room and greeted by a large jolly monk with an infectious smile. He wore simple but clean robes and had the appearance of Santa Claus – but, of course, without any hair. While the others bowed to him (as is traditional), he rushed over to shake my hand. He had very big hands that covered mine and he hugged me with a gracious welcome. As he motioned for us to sit, a novice brought tea and water on a tray and set them in front of us. He folded his hands in his lap and said, "Now, what can I do for you?" I explained that I was in Myanmar to learn and that I wanted to know about his school.

Over the next two hours we visited about his school and my research on politics and religion. In several different ways and different points in the conversation, he told me that we have an obligation and responsibility to help those in need. After our visit, he gave me tour of his school which was home to more than two-thousand homeless Myanmar children. As we walked through dormitories of children he spoke to them as a father would walking past his child's bedroom. Some he would chat with about school work, others he would laugh with about some inside joke, and he would playfully wake some who were sleeping. The children very obviously adored him as did his staff of monks and nuns. It reminded me of walking the hallways with a well-loved school headmaster. The children in his care were abandoned – many dropped off at the entrance of the monastery as infants. They slept on bamboo mats on cots stacked two and three levels high or on the floors. He forbade the young children to collect alms saying, "he wanted them in school, and being out collecting alms prevented them from learning." He told me that he allows the infants to be adopted, but that he has strict rules about who he allows to adopt the children. I was stunned by the man's work. With the support of donors, he is providing holistic care for the world's neediest and most vulnerable humans. When we first sat down to visit, he told me that he felt inadequate because he did not have a "secular education." When we shook hands in parting, it was I who felt inadequate. I was in awe of his work and stunned by the magnitude of the need. With very little resources, no material rewards or creature comforts, this man was caring for the those who need it the very most.

Part of the culture shock for me was rooted in poverty shock. I experienced this phenomenon in Vietnam and Cambodia, but in Myanmar I lived with and regularly met people who lived on about $200 USD or less a year. The hardships and challenges my neighbors and friends experienced on a daily basis were overwhelming. I did not travel to Myanmar to "save the people," but my heart was often heavy with the poverty and I felt helpless. It did not seem that my work (teaching) was really making a difference. The powerlessness was disheartening. My Myanmar friends assured me that I was helping and my teaching and research would in time make an impact on the lives of the Myanmar community. Also, I hope that this book is a way to help. In a visit with US Ambassador Derek Mitchell, he said "if we could just get others to see that a few million dollars we are now spending elsewhere would make a world of difference for the people and democracy of Myanmar."

Leaning In

Sometimes the best way to handle a tough problem like culture shock, is to lean in to it. So to battle the culture shock, I took off my shoes and put on flip flops and leaned in. I stopped fighting the traffic and the time it took me to accomplish the tasks on my list. I pushed myself on into a daily routine. I put myself out there – in the culture and with people. I made mistakes, laughed at myself, and apologized when needed. I made my bed every morning, shopped the local markets, and cooked my meals. I stopped fighting the pace of the pedestrians on the sidewalk. I started carrying an umbrella to block the sun and the rain. The smells not only became familiar, but I stopped noticing them at all. My skin began to adjust and over the next weeks and months I begin to feel not only like I had adjusted, but like I belonged. I no longer felt oddly out of place. By engaging and developing my own daily routine, I had come to adapt to the new environment. Over time, I learned what to expect in most situations. I learned how to deal with the taxi drivers and appreciated the new classroom norms. I adapted and learned to welcome new ways of thinking and attitudes. Once I had mentally processed my culture shock and adapted, I still found that I was perpetually the "foreigner." The term "foreigner" is commonly used by the Myanmar people. When you arrive in the Yangon airport at immigration, you find that your choices are "Myanmar Citizen" or "Foreigner."

Foreigners

The term "foreigner" is loaded with political meaning and history in Myanmar. Sadly, it does not simply mean that you are a stranger in a strange land, a land that you are just visiting, but rather it carries pejorative connotations. The term is directed squarely at exclusion and at defining "others." You are not one of us. As such, the "foreigner" status is a highly sensitive and politically charged matter in Myanmar. Unwanted foreign influence or the "foreigner problem" is still a common concern (in part because of unfounded fears of the small Muslim minority). Foreign clothes, films, foods, names, ideas, religions, institutions, businesses, and even Fulbright scholars are questioned and resisted by many in Myanmar. In June 2016, I gave a public lecture on religion and politics and during the question and answer session was politely told, "I do not agree with your foreign ideas." This attitude is, in no small part, a result of colonization. The Burmese people were subjected to not one, but two colonial powers. The British and the

Japanese both exerted complete foreign control over the country as recently as the 1940s. These colonial authorities interfered and regulated Burmese life to an astonishing degree. For example, the British even oversaw domestic disputes and colonial medical authorities demanded that Burmese children be vaccinated in a different manner than had been routinely done in Burma at that time.

Chettyars

In 2015, every time I asked a monk or community leader about foreigners and conflict, I was told the story of Indian moneylenders (called Chettyars). The Chettyars were Indian money lenders (not really banks, just family networks) who made loans at low interest rates to Burmese farmers between 1900 and the 1930s. Although their primary goal was not to foreclose on the Burmese farms, they frequently ended up with the farm land when the farmers were unable to repay their debts. Between 1900 and the Great Depression, significant amount of Burmese land was handed over to the Indian Chettyars. The Chettyars are especially despised today, and seen as another example of unwanted foreign interference in Myanmar's domestic affairs.

Kala

At their mother's knees and in school, Myanmar children are taught metta, merit, and about the wonders of their country's ancient kings and revered Buddhist monks. When speaking about their country they almost always begin with King Anawrahta. Anawrahta is seen as the country's founder. In 1044, he established the first Burmese empire that formed the basis of modern-day Myanmar. Myanmar people often also reference to King Thibaw. Thibaw was the last king of Burma. Just before the final battle with the British, King Thibaw himself donned a suit of armor and announced to his people that he would march with his army to expel the English heretics, the "kala," and uphold the religion and honor of the Burmese people. His fight with the British ended in disaster, but today he is remembered for fighting the foreigners and "kala." Thibaw's removal was the end of an era for the people of Myanmar and the beginning of an era of struggle to return what many Myanmar citizens believe they once were.

The word "kala" used by King Thibaw, is today commonly used as a degrading and abusive term in Myanmar. During colonial days, the Burmese used the phrase "bo kyet chee kala" ("shit-colored Indians who think they are British") to refer to the Indians. Today, kala or kalar is hateful slang for outsider, foreigner, or alien. Westerners are sometimes referred to as "white kala." The term is most commonly used a demeaning insult for anyone dark skinned, usually of Muslim or of Indian origin, by Myanmar people who believe themselves to be wholly Burmese. Muslims in Myanmar regularly suffer social and religious discrimination. Although the term has other meanings, it is often used in hateful, racist, and degrading manner such as "saut kalar" (dick-head kalar) and "khwe kalar" (dog kalar) when referring to people of the Muslim faith. One of my Muslim students told me that when he was a child and teenager that other children and adults would often call him a "sout kalar" ("shitty kalar"). They would tell him to go back to a "kalar country" where he was from and that he did not belong in Myanmar since they considered it to be a Buddhist country (more on this later). Not that it made any difference to those who were taunting him, but his family has been in Myanmar for many generations.

Allegiance to a Foreign Power

The military government refused to acknowledge the results of the election in 1990 and spent considerable effort afterward working to weaken the National League for Democracy (NLD). Not only did they target the NLD, but specifically began a public campaign aimed at Daw Aung San Suu Kyi. The government claimed that she was awarded the Nobel Peace Prize because she was a "follower they [the West] had raised." The military leaders said that they would "never accept the leadership of a person under foreign influence who will dance to the tune of a foreign power." In the government controlled press, the military suggested that she did not represent the people of Myanmar, but instead represented "foreign imperialist powers who continue their habit of brutally bullying the weak and interfering shamelessly in the internal affairs of other countries."

The military, which kept Daw Suu under house arrest for nearly two decades, has never wanted her to have a chance at the presidency and has used the "foreigner issue" against her. Even though her party won a landslide victory again 2015, Daw Suu is not and cannot officially be the president of Myanmar, because she married a "foreigner" and her two sons are "foreigners." Myanmar's military written 2008

Constitution (Article 59f) drafted by the military, prevents Daw Suu from being president because of her "allegiance to a foreign power." Daw Suu's late husband was British and her two sons are British citizens.

In 2016, Daw Suu is running her country. She holds the title of State Counselor and is operating above the office of the president. However, many of the Myanmar people still harbor a distinct fear and a long history of worry about foreigners which dates back centuries and is a common part of the culture.

Looking Deeply

My daughter, a 20-year-old college sophomore, joined me in Thailand and Myanmar for a few weeks in January of 2016. We raced through seven Thai universities in the span of a few days. I was giving lectures on democracy, religion, and an open society, and she was taking it all in and making friends. Once in Myanmar, we walked the streets of Yangon seeing the sights and taking in the history, culture, and pagodas. She taught a few English classes at the university where I was teaching and we made trips into the countryside to see local life.

My gracious and kind daughter was friended by a nine-year-old girl who works in the Bogyoke Aung San Market. The very large market, fashioned in colonial architecture, was built by the British in 1926 (the British called it Scott's Market). My daughter's young friend sold fans, postcards, and directed customers to specific stalls. In 2016, child labor is sadly too common in Myanmar.

Everywhere we went, my daughter was treated like a celebrity. Many people stopped her and asked if she would pose for a photo with them. People would point from buses. Taxi drivers would stare. It was very uncomfortable for her. So I finally asked my Myanmar friends why she was being treated so. Several explained that seeing a young beautiful foreign woman was very uncommon and that for many people in Myanmar, she was one of the first they had ever seen in person. Another explained the staring by saying, "we've never see such foreigners and we must look deeply." Myanmar in 2016 was still just beginning to open the doors to world, so for many people in this very isolated land, my beautiful daughter was indeed a rare sight that required "looking deeply."

I believe that the "foreigner" status and concept of "othering" is something that the people of Myanmar must process and find some resolution. The "foreigner issue" has created significant conflict and discord. Fifty years of isolation have allowed the Myanmar people precious little opportunity to consider how they will interact with "others." The people of Myanmar are only just today beginning to understand the interdependence and connections that bind all humans to one another on this pale blue dot. As a traveler, as a visitor, you will be openly and warmly welcomed in Myanmar. Indeed, it was the kindness and the generosity of the Myanmar people that made the transition from culture-shocked-American to at-ease-adapted-expat significantly less difficult. Those days when I felt awkward and lost, my Myanmar friends extended a saving line of sincere kindness and warm generosity.

Winds of Change

The people of Myanmar are living in a whirlwind of change in 2016. Coffee and rice production are bringing income into the rice bowl once again. The future is brighter, provided that the leaders and world leaders will seize the moment. They must not shrink in fear and isolationism. Looking at the faces of my students, I see hope. The National League for Democracy is working to engage with the outside world and is making progress toward changes in Myanmar's foreign policy. It is indeed a time of transition. Since 2011, Myanmar has markedly improved its relations with the wider international community. The new government has pursued an independent, non-aligned, and active foreign policy. Daw Suu also heads the Ministry of Foreign Affairs and she is departing from the defensive and inward-looking policies of the previous military administration. While Daw Suu has already greatly increased interaction with the outside world, I learned first-hand that struggle and suffering continue in Myanmar.

Robert Sterken with the head monk Sayadaw from
Aung Ze Yar Min Monastery and U Htoo Htoo Wah (2016).

Rowing the Rangoon River (2016). Photo credit: Robert Sterken.

Robert Sterken with Khin Sandar, Than Toe Aung, and Ju Ju Than (2016).

Chapter 3

Suffering and Struggle in the land of Pagodas

◊

Before the Mast

I had the good fortune to be born to loving parents in the United States. Unlike some, I do not believe that I earned that good fortune. I just arrived one hot night in July, in a Houston, Texas hospital. In spite of all of its faults, the United States offers its citizens a wonderful range of privileges. Yes, Americans can and should aspire to do better. While I fully agree that there is much that needs changing, American children do have access to basic healthcare and, even if not optimal, almost all have educational opportunities. Americans do not have to live in quiet fear. Even in times of bitter nationalism and extreme patriotism, most Americans are (mostly) safe to write, speak, and worship (or not) as they choose. American passports are welcomed by more countries than almost any other passport. Americans, for the most part, are free. Unlike many people, US citizens are free to travel almost anywhere in the world. From my American life and land of privilege, I took my United States passport and went out into the world. Like Henry David Thoreau, "I did not wish to take a cabin passage, but rather to go before the mast and on the deck of the world." I wanted to feel the rains and see the pagodas. I wanted to meet the people and learn of their lives, joys, and struggles.

In Myanmar and more generally across Southeast Asia I witnessed suffering. In Cambodia I reverently visited the Killing Fields and learned of unimaginable horrors that took place on that land. In Thailand, I had dinner with Her Royal Highness Princess Maha Chakri Sirindhorn, learned of the suffering of her aging father, and saw a very repressive Thai government. In Vietnam I witnessed a country recovering from decades of fighting. In Myanmar, I saw the devastating effects on the people and infrastructure of fifty years of brutal and harsh military rule. Those long years of ruthless military rule have had a deep and soul changing impact on the people. They suffered and are suffering, but it did not destroy their spirit and their hopes for the future.

On November 8, 2015, Alison and I took part in an election party at the United States American Center in Yangon. The American Center is a beautiful building owned and operated by the US State Department. It has meeting rooms, free Wi-Fi, offers regular courses, shows movies, and maintains a substantial library. Myanmar high school and college students regularly meet at the American Center for different staff organized activities. The election day event was a grand party, marked by crepe paper streamers, balloons, and lots of good will and cheer. The students who were not old enough to vote in the actual election were given an opportunity to vote in a mock election of American cartoon figures, (Captain America won over Superman). The Deputy Chief of the US Embassy spoke about the historic Myanmar vote and the US Ambassador's wife joined in the festivities. I spoke about the nature of democracy. I did not want to be "professor doom" but I did want to express a note of caution. The Myanmar people had such giddy and perhaps unrealistically high hopes that I worried about the inevitable letdown. Change would not occur overnight; even if the vote pushed out the military rulers, real life changes would take time, even decades to take place.

The Myanmar people have long sought freedom and an open democratic society, at least since the time that the British ruled their country. After throwing off the yoke of the colonial powers, at first the British and then the Japanese in the 1940s, it seemed that they were well on their way to reaching that goal, when the country was taken over by a ruthless military junta. In 1988 and then again in the early 1990s the people strongly and loudly demanded their civil rights and democratic change. The leader for this change was and is Daw Aung San Suu Kyi. Daw Suu, (Mother Suu) as she is affectionately known, and her National League for Democracy party won the elections in 1990 in a huge and historic landside. The military leaders were surprised with the landslide victory, decided not to honor the 1990 vote, and instead placed Daw Suu under house arrest for the next eighteen years and sent thousands of others to prison.

When Alison and I arrived in Myanmar a month before the election, the US Embassy and everyone else in the country had no idea who might win the 2015 elections or if the military might react as they did in the 1990 elections, ignore the election results, and severely punish anyone who protested. The people were still fearful of a similar and potential military crackdown. The Embassy warned expats to stay away from political rallies and gatherings. That proved very hard to do as the rallies were quite mobile. Trucks with banners, bands, and candidates roamed the streets and stopped seemingly at random. The military ruling party (USDP) used the police to trap the people around the trucks in order to create an instant crowd for the cameras. Alison and I found ourselves in several of these rallies as we walked the streets shopping or taking in the sights of the city.

The 2015 election was thrilling and eagerly anticipated, in part because the people of Myanmar had so long and so greatly suffered under the military government. Under the military regime, the country's economic situation was dismal. By the time of the 88 uprising, widespread government corruption, extreme poverty, and nationwide food shortages were common. As stated earlier, during the 88 uprising the military killed at least three thousand Myanmar citizens (including monks), put many in prison, and displaced hundreds of thousands more. In the 1990s and into the early 2000s the military government isolated and denied the citizens of Myanmar basic social, civil, and economic rights.

In 2007, thousands of Myanmar's monks protested and many were killed and put in prison. In her book, *Freedom from Fear*, Daw Suu wrote about the suffering brought by the fear of living under such a military government. "Within a system which denies the existence of basic human rights, fear tends to be the order of the day. Fear of imprisonment, fear of torture, fear of death, fear of losing friends, family, property or means of livelihood, fear of poverty, fear of isolation, fear of failure. A most insidious form of fear is that which masquerades as common sense or even wisdom, condemning as foolish, reckless, insignificant or futile the small, daily acts of courage which help to preserve man's self-respect and inherent human dignity. It is not easy for a people conditioned by fear under the iron rule of the principle that might is right to free themselves from the enervating miasma of fear. Yet even under the most crushing state machinery courage rises up again and again, for fear is not the natural state of civilized man."

Students, Fears, and Opportunity

I set aside time to interview each of my Myanmar students. I wanted to get to know them as individuals, so I spent about twenty minutes (depending on the student) asking them questions about their lives, plans, family, and dreams. I made notes as we visited (I also do this with my American students). Many were hesitant, as this interview required them to sit with a professor and to speak in English. It turned out to be one of the most rewarding experiences of my time in Myanmar. Meeting with so many children (young adults) of Myanmar's mothers and fathers taught me a great deal about their lives in shadows of fear, and about their hopes, and dreams. I learned stories of courage and inspiration that made me feel delight, a delight in being in the presence of such wonder. Every single student had exciting plans; music, social work, policy making, business, farming, teaching, journalism, and writing poetry. Two students told me they were going to open a Christian school for homeless children.

The interviews were upbeat and pleasant, but I also noted two heart wrenching undertones. First, nearly every student told me that they would like to go on for more education, but unless they could find a foreign scholarship they would not have the opportunity. Their families could not afford to send them abroad for an education and there are no real opportunities for such in Myanmar (more on that in chapter six). For an ever optimistic educator this was difficult for me to hear and accept. I wanted to help these students, but there was nothing I could really do.

Second, many of these students (from the one hundred and fifty or so that I interviewed) told me that they would be working to take care of their parents and extended family members. Many were already doing just that. One student who constantly asked brilliant questions, regularly stayed after class to ask me for reading material, was also working all day on the Yangon docks to support his parents and younger siblings. Early in the course, I asked my teaching assistant why his name was not on the roll sheet. Her reply, "Oh, he cannot afford to pay for the course fees." These students never missed a single class. They well understood the value of what too many American students have come to take for granted or see as simply a requirement for a degree.

The interviews revealed two other constant factors in these young people's lives. First, many told me that their parents had forbid them from participating in politics. When I asked why, they all had a similar reply, "politics is dangerous, one can get put in prison, or killed." As a parent myself, I sympathized with their parent's protective rule, but as a political activist, I felt the need to call these young people into action against evil. I did not make such a call. Second, several of my student's parents had been or were at that time political prisoners. During one interview, a student started crying and told me that her father was currently in prison because of a Facebook post. Her father, Khum Jar Lee, had been charged with harming the image of the Myanmar military through a simple Facebook post. He had posted a cartoon about the military. A few months later (April 1, 2016) he was freed from Insein prison after completing a six-month sentence. The United States Embassy sent Deputy Chief of Mission Kristen Bauer to meet him as he was released.

Fulbrighter with a Heavy Heart

The suffering and struggles of the people of Myanmar were all too real and weighed heavily on my heart. My Myanmar friends consoled me with the idea that I was making a difference by teaching and bringing light to a place that had long been dark and isolated. Their words were encouraging, but to a future Fulbrighter or to anyone who takes on these issues and concerns, I would strongly advise first learning and adopting the resilient coping mechanisms of the people of Myanmar.

Many of the Myanmar people are keenly aware of the difference between pain and suffering. Knowing that difference gives them resilience, hope, and even some measure of control over their lives. Pain is something a person experiences when hurt. For example, the hurt felt from the loss of a loved one is pain. The death causes the pain, and it hurts. A person has little or no control over the pain. Pain is inevitable. Suffering, however, is different from pain. Suffering is one's reaction to the hurt. A person does have, at least some measure, of control over suffering. We can choose the response to the pain in our lives. A citizen (and his family) who has been put in prison for a Facebook post, feels pain. His reaction to the injustice, for example, becoming angry, planning revenge, or feeling depressed, are all beyond the pain, those reactions constitute the suffering. Many of the people of Myanmar have chosen to accept the pain (at least when it is beyond their control) and to reject the suffering.

That important distinction, understanding the choice about suffering, helped me in a number of ways during my time in Myanmar. I live in a privileged world. I had the ever present luxury of boarding a giant airliner and returning to Texas. For me, no small measure of guilt accompanied that privilege. My time in Myanmar provided me with extraordinary examples of true suffering and struggle, like those the Myanmar people have faced for the last fifty plus years. It also revealed many unearned privileges, advantages of birth, missed creature comforts of home, and daily reminders of how different life actually is in Myanmar.

Changed Plans and Struggle

The very structure and composition of my days changed, once I was settled into life in Myanmar. I am an organized, detailed, and extremely goal oriented person. I am a planner. I make lists. I have expectations of myself. I have detailed specific outcomes for how the days, weeks, months, years, and even decades of my life will unfold. That's just how I operate. I had planned and hoped for the Fulbright for years. I have running plans (I am a long-distance runner) for each day, month, year, and decade. I have specific steps for achieving those plans penciled in for each week and day. The structure of the culture, timing of the people of Myanmar, and pace of life forced changes. I suffered and struggled with those outside forces. I chastised myself when I accomplished only a few things each day from the list of things I set out to accomplish.

Everything (and that is not an overstatement) in Myanmar seemed hard. My normal pace of ticking off many items on my list each day came to a screeching halt. Every seemingly simple task was a struggle. Yes, there are solutions to these struggles, but the solutions forced changes in my expectations. I had to look at everything as a new adventure. I longed for my life in Texas. Yes, despite the longing, the entire adventure was a rare and extraordinary gift. It is indeed, "the gig of a lifetime," but that does not negate that fact that living in Burma was a struggle – for me – in many small and in some significant ways. Washing clothes, washing dishes, cashing a check, running, walking to the market, writing an email, cooking dinner, making coffee, even picking up a form from a government office demanded a heretofore unrequired level of patience and involved frustrating delays, hassles, modifications, and compromise that brought important life lessons.

The very basic element of washing dishes (and fruits and vegetables) was difficult at first. I have a close Cambodian friend who is very strict about boiling water before each and every use. He drilled that lesson home with his own daughter and inadvertently with me. I was worried about getting my dishes, fruits, and vegetables clean. There was no hot water in our kitchen. So for the first few weeks, Alison and I dutifully boiled water before washing. This was a significant hassle, so we eventually just stopped all of the boiling and began to wash food and dishes in the tap water. I thought, "I'd have to be really unlucky to get sick in such a way." It took my body about a month to become accustomed to the new demands, but it ultimately adjusted.

Washing clothes was different. Drying clothes was often impossible due to the high humidity. Wash-and-wear was a misnomer. The washing machine in my apartment was absolutely violent with my clothes. Shirts came out of the wash looking like that had been stretched between three oddly placed poles. Shirt collars were destroyed. When dressed in these "laundered clothes," it appeared that I was wearing cotton sacks that were coming apart at the seams. There are very few clothes dryers in Myanmar. There was not one in our apartment, so clothing had to be hung up for drying, which in the tropical heat rendered my shirts and pants oddly board stiff and wrinkled in a way that even made ironing difficult.

Drying in the rainy season was even more of a challenge. Clothes washed and hung up on Saturday morning remained damp on Monday or even Tuesday, and they had acquired a sickly, sour, aroma. There was so much water in the air that it would not evaporate from the dishes in the drying rack, much less from cotton shirts and towels. A simple item on my to-do list, laundry was difficult, frustrating, and a struggle.

As a runner, I am accustomed to walking out my front door in Tyler, Texas, setting my Garmin to the nearest satellite, and taking off on a safe route for as many miles as I planned for that day. I typically run between five and fifteen miles a day. I attempted to maintain this pattern in our first days in Yangon only to be exasperated and discouraged. The heat I could manage (but my fair skin did suffer from the searing rays of the tropical heat and sun), but the exhaust from the many unregulated cars (in the glaring absence of any semblance of an environmental protection agency), buses, trucks, and burgeoning industries left the roadside air hard to breath. I bought a mask, but, I found it hard to breathe in the mask. The most significant challenge to running any distance in Yangon turned out to be the dismal condition of the roads and sidewalks. The roads are extremely crowded with cars, people pushing carts, and rickshaws, and the sidewalks are terribly dangerous. The sidewalks – where they exist – are built up about a foot or more from the roadway. So one has to jump or step up and down at every intersection and driveway. Challenging but again, okay, this is all part of the adventure. But the sidewalks are also crowded with people and more importantly they are very often missing rather large sections of concrete at random and unexpected intervals. In places where the concrete slab is missing, there is usually a three or four-foot deep hole revealing pipes, garbage, and the underworld. In short, running at any pace for a long distance was extremely challenging and dangerous. Eventually, I joined the United States Embassy American Club so that I could use the gym and treadmill. I logged 1,226 treadmill miles during my Myanmar days. In Texas, I normally log about 1,700 miles a year. Getting to the American Club was also a significant daily adventure. The club was only three miles from our apartment, but the journey took about thirty or forty minutes by taxi. Some days I just walked.

Walking the Yangon sidewalks was itself a lesson in habit and culture. I learned that I walk fast – in comparison to slower pace of the people in Yangon. Perhaps it is because of the heat, or maybe it's the flip-flops, or the longyi's, or the ever present umbrellas, but many Myanmar people walk slowly. I was told by Myanmar people who live outside the city that "Yangon city people walk too fast." On the crowded sidewalks it is almost impossible to go around or pass people, so one is forced to join in the local pace and slow down.

The pace of the day is often also slowed by the frequent power outages. The electricity was as a matter of routine not available for hours at a time several times each week (sometimes several times a day). It was a surreal experience to be sitting on the balcony, writing on my laptop and watching the entire city go dark. Until backup generators engage, the Wi-

Fi is unavailable when the power is off, as are all traffic lights. Traffic lights are set to such extremely long intervals that it is normal for a taxi driver to put the car in park and turn off the engine at an intersection, leaving you sweating in the sun in the back seat in your tent-like cotton sack. Such are the forced adjustments and frustrations I faced.

Getting A Visa and Renewing Forms

Getting a tourist visa for a thirty day Myanmar visit is a simple task that only takes a few minutes online. Obtaining a visa for a long stay Myanmar is quite the opposite. It is no simple task. In fact, of the five US Fulbright Scholars who would be journeying to Myanmar for 2015 and 2016 all had widely varying experiences and each paid significantly different fees for our visas. The US Embassy in Yangon worked hard to secure a visa for me. In September 2015, the Embassy in Yangon received Ministry of Education permission for me to enter the country to teach at a private college, Myanmar Institute of Theology. Even with Myanmar Immigration authorization (I had the letter of approval) I still had trouble actually obtaining a visa. In the end, I had to mail my passport to the Myanmar Embassy in Washington DC along with $180 for a "Business Visa," that was valid only for thirty days (a regular tourist visa is valid for the same thirty days and is one hundred dollars cheaper). The US Embassy said that I/we would attempt to obtain an extended visa once in the country. Despite the hassle, it turned out that I was fortunate to be granted entry as all, as other scholars remained outside of Myanmar for months and months while waiting for approval and a visa. I would later pay

$320 for a year-long visa, but it would come with some unusual requirements. The year-long visa required a Myanmar Foreigners Registration Certificate (FRC).

Frustrations and Paperwork

In my first days in country I wondered why everything I tried do in Myanmar took so long. Each day, I set out to accomplish my usual list – and at the end of each day I found that I was moving things to the next day. This following story may help explain some of the reason for my productivity – or lack thereof.

On the morning of December 14, 2015, after being in Myanmar for roughly two months, I set out to retrieve my FRC form. This is an actual piece of paper, used by Myanmar Immigration. Every foreigner who has stayed in Myanmar more than 90 days must be issued a Foreigner's Registration Certificate (FRC) according to the "Foreigner's law." One must have this FRC piece of paper in hand in order to leave the country. When one leaves Myanmar the immigration officer takes the form from you, stamps it is a few places, writes on it, and then sends it to the main office. You must – in person – retrieve that same actual piece of paper from the immigration office in downtown Yangon. Don't ask me why, I do not know.

On the day I set out to pick up the form, I walked to Insein Road to catch a taxi at about 10:00am. After being turned away by two drivers, I found one who said he knew where I want to go and that he would take me there for 4000 kyats ($4). I climbed into the backseat of the taxi and the driver turned off the motor. We sat. We waited. We waited for the light at the next cross roads (about a quarter of a mile away) to change. After about fifteen minutes the driver restarted his Toyota Corolla and we were off – to the next junction that is – where we sat again and waited. Google said it should take about twenty-four minutes' drive to the immigration office from our apartment, yet it took about an hour.

At about 11:00 am, the driver dropped me about two blocks from my destination. But no worries. I walked. It took me a while to find the street as it was not marked. Following on my phone, Google announced that I had arrived. I look around for what might be an official government office. Nothing. The only markings were the street numbers above the doorway – 122. I cautiously entered the dirty lime-green hallway and then entered a stairway. I was told by people descending the staircase that I was in the right place to obtain an FRC form. There was a small group of monks at the top of the stairs – I said, "good morning," as I passed, and they laughed. At the top of the stairs I found a very large and open office. It was full of people, maybe a hundred, waiting. I thought, "oh...no." There were papers everywhere! Stacks and stacks of papers piled on desk after desk. I asked, "FRC form?" and was pointed to a desk where a woman was eating her lunch. I awkwardly waited while she ate.

At 11:45, the immigration officer took a break from eating her lunch. I apologized for interrupting her meal. She did not seem to understand me. She took my passport and turned to a wall of file cabinets behind her desk. She pulled out a brown folder that held hundreds of pages of paper. She flipped through the papers. After about five minutes she arrived at mine. She did not speak to me during any of her search. She then wrote on another form and said, "go pay." I looked around. Where? Who? She pointed toward the door but gave no other directions. I walked toward the door worrying about leaving my passport on her desk. Inquiring about where to pay, I walked back down the stairs; the monks were of no help. I walked down the dark staircase looking for a cashier to pay.

At 11:50am, I finally discovered the window marked "cash in" and took my place in line. After waiting for about fifteen minutes, I reached the window and was told the office only accepts USD which required search for an ATM. I walked down the street and finally came across an ATM machine. I put my card in the machine. Nothing. The machine appeared to be operating but did not acknowledge my card. A police officer standing next to me said, "broke." Fortunately, the machine spit out my card. At 12:05pm, I found a "money changer" and attempted to change Myanmar Kyat to USD. After some struggle the clerk finally understood and I was given $10 USD cash in the denomination of two five dollar bills. I worried as I walk back to the Immigration office that they would not like the bills, as they were not pristine. At 12:15, I again stood in line again and then handed the two bills to the cashier. She examined each bill very carefully, for so long that I thought she was surely going to hand them back to me rejecting them, but she finally decided to accept them.

At 12:20, I walked back up to the first floor and gave the receipt to the woman who had possession of my passport the receipt. Again, no words were exchanged. She then took my passport and the FRC form to another woman at another desk. There they worked with yet another governmental official else for about ten minutes. Then they both wrote information into a big green ledger book. Line by line, she carefully wrote information from my FRC form into the ledger – along with thousands and thousands of others. Finally, at 12:30, I walked out of the Immigration office with my FRC form. As I walked out, I looked across the street and saw an ancient British colonial building emblazoned with the words "Government Telegraph Office." Seems about right, I think. I have been told that one can actually still send a telegram. I took a photo of the telegraph office and wondered to whom would I send a telegram to and what it might say.

To reward myself for surviving, I treated myself to a quick but excellent lunch at the Rangoon Tea House, followed by an hour long taxi ride back to our apartment. At 1:35 pm, I arrived at my apartment. With a good portion of the day consumed, I had only retrieved my FRC form, eaten lunch, but had accomplished precious little else. As frustrating as these things were, I was able to adjust – over time. I slowed down. I put fewer expectations on myself for each day. I relaxed a bit. I also came to understand something new about these frustrations. A few of my fellow Fulbrighter's labeled these frustrations as having a "Burma day." Meaning they blamed the country, culture, and what many people frustratingly called "the Burmese way" of doing things. Many Myanmar people apologized for their "backward Burmese ways." I think it is erroneous and even harmful to transfer these frustrations to our hosts. Without any doubt, we all have frustrations with many things (slow store clerks, lost packages, banking issues and on and on) in the United States and elsewhere every day. Yes, the Myanmar culture reshaped my behavior, but I did not let that reshaping make me unhappy – for long. Yes, many days were frustrating and even bad – but they are sometimes so in Texas too – so I did not let get me down or blame it on the "Burmese way."

Struggling for Democracy

I gave a series of public lectures in Thailand with United States Ambassador Glyn T. Davies about democracy, elections, and an open society. The Ambassador and I both spoke for twenty or so minutes about the American democracy and the importance of rule of law and human rights. In the question and answer sessions that followed, the Ambassador often left for another appointment and I stayed to answer questions from the audience. The audiences were mostly college students and they had a number insightful questions. Their country was under the rule of a harsh and unforgiving military government and they were worried. Toward the end of one of the question and answer sessions, a student stood up in the back of the room and the staff person provided him with a mic. He started off hesitantly and slowly, but then asked a question I will never forget. He described the struggle for basic rights, such as the right to speak openly, then asked, "how long should we wait for our rights?" And then added, "how long should we wait before we take to the streets?" There I was, an American professor who believes strongly in human rights, in democracy, and in respect for all people, faced with a student who wanted to know when to fight for those rights. How long should he wait? How would you have answered? Would you tell a twenty-something college student to risk prison or maybe even death in the streets of Bangkok for his civil rights?

I responded like a father, not like an activist professor. I said, "look to your neighbors in Myanmar, they have long struggled for their rights. For decades they have struggled and suffered and today they reap the rewards as their democracy is now blooming. They have worked and struggled since 1962 for democracy. Daw Aung San Suu Kyi struggled alongside her people from 1988 to November 2015." "Yes," I replied, "do what you safely can, but be cautious, safe, and remember that you could be in for a long struggle. Great things are worth great struggle." He sat down, seemingly disappointed with my response. I went on to answer more questions. But met his eyes a few more times and could see the sadness. While his struggle for his basic rights was in every way real, my answers were delivered from the vantage point of someone with an American passport who would be boarding on a jumbo jet and returning to the land of the free.

All of the small personal struggles I faced in living and working in Myanmar do not at all compare to the fifty years of struggle that the people of that country have endured. My struggles and small achievements, in no way compare to the superhuman accomplishments of Daw Aung Suu Kyi. Her struggle and sacrifice brought democracy the country and hope to her people. Those real challenges were long and difficult. Many people died in Insein Prison. The key point here is that the accomplishments came as a result of accepting the consequences of the sacrifices inherent in achieving those accomplishments. Daw Suu was willing to give up her family life, her own personal freedom, and live in decades of isolation, all to support her nation's fight to rid itself of military rule. Was her sacrifice worth the losses? Was the struggle worth it? Only she can answer those questions. Through her example, it is clear that it is through the long battle, the long struggle, that we earn the results.

If I could visit with that Thai student again, I would tell him that his life, like Daw Suu's life, will not be determined by an easy shortcut to the rights he desires for himself and his people but rather will be determined by the determination he and others are willing and able to sustain in order to win the long good fight. Daw Suu meditated, painted, played her piano in an isolated struggle for seventeen years. She endured the stresses, isolation, loss of her family, and the uncertainty of house arrest all so that ultimately she would on November 8, 2015 see a landslide democratic election win in Myanmar. I am not saying that there is no success without pain. I am saying that real accomplishments such as bringing human rights to one's people, writing your book, running a marathon, earning a college degree, dancing on Broadway, and on and on, require accepting pain and the inevitable daunting risks, realizing that suffering is a choice, and accepting the struggle as a significant component of success.

Simplicity, Struggle, and Success

The daily trials and frustrations I faced forced me to live more simply and with patience, tolerance, and acceptance. Although, Yangon is thousands of miles from Concord, I found myself thinking a great deal about Thoreau's attempt to live simply. The structure of my Myanmar life required me to simplify. As I studied monk's lives, I came to know just how simply one can live. Monks and nuns lead very simple and uncomplicated lives that are largely free of things such as personal property. They are allowed to have eight basic necessities. Although, as I said above, I visited many monks and nuns who owned a long list of things, I saw monks with laptops and I did not see meet any who did not own a cell phone.

For the monastic, the simple life remains the goal as Buddhist monks and nuns typically only possess the following personal property: 1) an outer robe, 2) an inner robe, 3) a thick double robe for winter (which is nonexistent in southern Myanmar), 4) an alms bowl for gathering food, 5) a razor for shaving, 6) a needle and thread, 7) a belt, and 8) a water strainer for removing impurities from drinking water. That's it. All one really needs are those eight items and metta. We also must have loving kindness.

In life, one needs kindness. The struggles of the people of Myanmar, Thailand, and my own taught me that, at least in part, one survives struggle and difficult circumstances through kindness. In order to survive one absolutely must practice being kind to oneself. Without it, we wither and die. Being kind to one's self is not something Americans are typically taught.

It was in my American yoga practice that my teachers first introduced the idea to me, but it was not until I had spent several months grappling with almost everything in Myanmar, that I come to fully realize the importance of kindness in one's challenges. While kindness is critical to success, so is struggle. We must be willing to struggle or fight to accomplish the difficult task. To run a marathon, write a book, earn a degree, raise good children, or to achieve democracy for the people of Myanmar requires real and long-term struggle. When I faced hard days in Myanmar I tried to remember to be kind to myself and to accept the struggle as the price of achieving my goals. Being a foreigner in a foreign land was hard, really difficult some days, some weeks, it was a struggle, but the rewards were immense.

Robert Sterken under the Bodhi tree (2015).
Photo credit: Alison Johnson Sterken.

Chapter 4

Monks with Cigars, Kindness, and Beer

◊

Chanting Daily Prayers

The Yangon city streets are largely free of taxis, buses, and people and are all quiet by nine or ten each night. I am sure that there is a nightlife somewhere in the city, but unlike London or Houston this city of five million sleeps. Perhaps it is because of the birds. Myanmar is home to an extraordinary number of birds, a total of 1062 species to be exact (by comparison the United States has 888). Myanmar is a birders' paradise. All of those birds, especially the crows, are noisy at the break of dawn. A German professor I worked with complained every time I saw him about the crows waking him each morning. The crows were also very noisy at dusk each evening. Maybe the citizens of Myanmar go to sleep early because they start each day far earlier than most humans. The tropical heat is less intense in the early hours and the people take advantage of the cooler morning air. Markets are teaming with shoppers just after dawn. Perhaps the city sleeps because every morning begins very early, in unison with the monks chanting. Theravada Buddhist monks begin their days with chanting their daily prayers. The chant is a form of musical verse or incantation that monks use to prepare for meditation. In the Theravada tradition, chanting is usually performed in Pali and chants are derived from the Pali Canon (a collection of Buddhist scriptures). A common chant is the Panca-sila, or the Five Precepts. The Five Precepts are taught to almost all Myanmar children.

The Five Precepts

I undertake to observe the precept to abstain from destroying living beings.
I undertake to observe the precept to abstain from taking things not given.
I undertake to observe the precept to abstain from sexual misconduct.
I undertake to observe the precept to abstain from false speech.
I undertake to observe the precept to abstain from liquor causing intoxication and heedlessness.
I undertake to observe the Five Precepts to the best of my ability.

Many mornings I awoke to monks chanting in a language I did not understand. After interviewing monks and after a great deal of reading, I learned that the monks practice a fairly typical set of chants. Among the most common is the Prayer of Mettā. The prayer of metta is a wish that all sentient beings (living beings) be well.

During my time in Myanmar, I adopted the prayer (in English) as my own mantra. Every morning while the monks chanted, I recited my own shortened version with them, "May all live in happiness. May all be safe. May all be healthy in mind and body. May all beings live in peace and harmony." Imagine waking every day of your life to such a chanted prayer. From not far beyond your bedroom window, one of the clergy of your village wakes you and your family with the good wishes of friendliness, consideration, kindness, and generosity. Every morning you are reminded of metta. After only a few months, I found that the daily, out loud expression of this prayer did help to further seat my desire that all sentient beings be well. Already a vegetarian, I even found myself skipping to avoid stepping on a beetle, and even wondering if I should kill the mosquito at my ankles in the elevator.

The Most Generous People on Earth

The London-based Charities Aid Foundation publishes an annual report titled the World Giving Index. The World Giving Index collects data on three specific charitable behaviors (not attitudes) from people around the world. The index notes citizen behavior with these three actions, within the last three months, 1) have you donated money to a charity, 2) volunteered time to an organization, and 3) helped a stranger or someone you didn't know who needed help? The most charitable people on our little planet live in Myanmar (Americans ranked second in the world). Being wealthy is obviously not a requirement for being generous. Every single day that I lived in Myanmar I was the recipient of the generous intentions of the people and I witnessed their generosity toward others. Shop owners would hurry to place items in the alms bowls of monks, nuns, and novices who were waiting patiently outside on the sidewalk.

Many citizens walking along the street would stop to put money in the bowl of a beggar. My students, university staff, and colleagues went out of their way to make sure I was taken care of and that had what I needed, not just for class, but things that I personally needed. They made sure I had dinner after late evening classes (they would often have a box of food waiting for me). A vendor I regularly visited would wave off my attempt to pay for a bottle of water. The water was her gift to me.

The security guard in my building regularly greeted me with a big smile and the traditional Myanmar greeting, "mingalaba." To say "mingalaba," is to give a kind blessing of joy and good wishes for prosperity. It is a very common greeting. Rather than greet with a "hello" or with a question, the greeter extends kindness and goodwill. Fellow faculty members regularly helped me with taxi drivers. After class, they would walk out to the street, hail a taxi, give the driver directions, and even negotiate a good price for me.

My Yangon University teaching assistants regularly brought me coffee before early morning classes and had breakfast waiting for me in my office after my 7:00am class. It is hard to detail the authentic sincerity of their generous spirits, but I believe that it is important to note that their behavior and actions were not a duty, but rather were sincere acts of kindness and generosity. When I asked my students to tell me what they were most proud of about their country, many told me they were proud of the "spirit of metta" and idea of "merit."

A Daily Practice

Monasteries are an integral part of life in Myanmar. The men, women, and children who live in them are completely dependent on the Myanmar people for all their material needs. Every day in the streets one sees monks and nuns gathering alms. Buddhist monks, nuns, and novices present themselves at the doorway of a home or shop and stand quietly and let their alms bowls be seen. The owner of the shop or house will place whatever he or she is able in the bowl (not money). The bowl in which the food is received and later eaten from is one of the eight requisites of monks and nuns (detailed the eight requisites in chapter three). The Myanmar people are indeed generous, for over half a million monks, nuns, and novices are dependent upon the generosity of others for their basic sustenance.

For the people of Myanmar, the practice of their religion is about action, the manner in which they behave toward themselves and others. Many of the people of Myanmar (not just the Buddhists) believe in "merit." Before considering merit, it is important to emphasize the word "practice." A practice denotes a regular habitual application or use of an idea or belief. The Myanmar people are the most authentically generous people on earth because they practice their beliefs every single day. Directly linked with metta (loving kindness) is the idea of merit. Merit is the result of good actions, deeds, or thoughts. Merit can be earned in a number of ways, but is a foundational to the generosity of the Myanmar people. Through good acts a person earns merit. Merit is thought to eventually bring a person closer to nirvana.

Merit also contributes to a person's immediate spiritual and physical life. Many Myanmar people believe that good actions, deeds, and even thinking good thoughts brings longevity, happiness in mind and body, bodily strength, and even wisdom. Of course, science supports their beliefs. Psychologists have written extensively about the positive individual and societal benefits of giving. Studies show that giving money to someone else makes a person far happier than if they had spent it on themselves. Other psychologists have found that giving has significant health benefits – even for people with chronic illnesses like AIDs or multiple sclerosis. The Myanmar people are living examples that giving promotes a sense of trust and cooperation. Crime, especially violent crime, rates are very low all across the country. Myanmar students often commented to me about how violent people are in the United States.

The earning of merit is contagious. When one Yangon citizen gives, she does not only help the immediate recipient, but also sends a ripple of generosity throughout her community. I experienced this over and over in Myanmar. The direct effect was that I too wanted to give. So every day when I set out to campus or to the market I would put Myanmar kyat in my right pocket (for easy access) to give to those begging on the streets. I regularly over tipped my taxi drivers and did all I could to make sure that they understood my good wishes for them. I bought treats for the maintenance men in my building (Alison actually started that practice with candy she brought from the US).

What can I do for you, my brother?

It was late. I was tired from a long day and three
hours of lecturing. As I paid my taxi driver, I
remembered that my fridge was nearly empty, Alison
was away traveling, and it was only Hjar Hjar at the
apartment. So carrying the dinner set out for me by
the staff, I went searching for a nearby shop that
would sell me a cold bottle of Myanmar beer. In
2016, there were not a lot choices of beer and no craft
beers were available. In addition to Myanmar beer,
Carlsberg sold its flagship beer as well as Tuborg and
Yoma, the latter a brand specifically brewed for the
Myanmar market. Heineken also produced and sold
four beer brands in Myanmar, but that was about all
that was available in 2016. Myanmar beer is nice light
bodied brew. It has a clear yellow color and a nice
aroma of sweet malts. It's a refreshing easy to drink
lager.

I came upon a shop with a crowd of people gathered
out front. Since it was a very small shop with the
entrance blocked by people, I stood outside peering in
to see if I might be able to spot a refrigerator that
might hold a bottle of cold beer. As I stood looking, a
man I had not seen spoke to me from the shadows
down near the sidewalk on the left side of the shop.
He was sitting in a small pink plastic chair. While
standing, he very kindly – in the King's English – he
asked, "what can I do for you, my brother?" I
explained about my search for cold bottle of
Myanmar beer. While pointing, he said, "no cold beer
here, you walk three shops down that way, and they
will have it for you." Something in the way he spoke,

the earnestness, that small act, and the kindness in his words was touching. It doesn't take much effort to practice metta.

Monks in Politics

Monks are among the primary teachers of metta and have long engaged directly in Myanmar politics. All of the monks I met were interesting men. Some smoked cigars and played chess. Most were very kind and soft spoken. Some were suspicious of me (wanting to know what I was writing). One wanted to know what I thought of him and if I was "judging him." Many were well read scholars. Several regularly travel the world giving lectures. Some were very talkative. I spent six hours sitting on the floor listening to one monk, while he was sitting on a large cushion. Many monks offered me food and soft drinks during the interviews. Some were angry (at their government). Some were even militant (angry at Muslims). I learned a great deal about their lives, religion, fears, and quests. I came to understand Theravada Buddhism in ways I never imagined.

When I asked my students to tell me their favorite story about a Myanmar monk, many wrote about U Ottama. Ottama was a prolific author and widely traveled scholar who took a leading role in the fight for Burmese independence from the British. Ottama was imprisoned several times by the British and while in prison, he went on a hunger strike, and died in 1939. U Ottama is widely considered one of Myanmar's national heroes. There is a park named after him in Yangon. Monks have clearly long been deeply involved in Burma's politics.

My research in Myanmar focused on religion and politics and is a book project separate from this one. In that "academic" book I report my research. To study religion and politics I needed to better and personally understand the dominant religion of the land. While the people of Myanmar claim many ethnic backgrounds, they are predominantly practicing Buddhists. The Myanmar government finally released the 2014 census data on July 21, 2016 (it was delayed for political reasons). Estimates still vary widely, but are that the country's population is reported to be about 75% Buddhist, 10% ethnoreligious (folk religions), 8% Christian (mostly Baptists), 4% Muslim, 2% Hindu, and a few others. In many ways the religious makeup of Myanmar is a mirror of that of the United States. One of the more significant similarities is that many people in the dominate religion are afraid of and intolerant of the tiny Muslim minority. There are vitriolic, hateful, and nationalistic monks who want to ban Muslim travel, expel Muslim citizens from the country, and who have led violent protests in Muslim communities.

Political science research shows that when a country's government adopts or strongly supports one specific religion, the larger society also tends to be less tolerant and more likely to violently discriminate against those who do not practice the dominate religion. Myanmar's government has for many centuries been closely linked with and has closely supported Theravada Buddhism.

In the 1960s, the military government decreed in the country's Constitution that Myanmar was a Buddhist country. That distinction has since been taken out of the Myanmar constitution, but still there remains a strong government regulation of religion and very strong government support for Buddhism. The government supports the religion financially and many of its leaders. Often those who suffer the most under a state established religions are those in the minority.

The minority Muslim population in Myanmar faces both government and social discrimination – and often violence. In June 2016, a group of Buddhist men from a village in central Myanmar destroyed a mosque. The men from the remote village about two-hours northeast of Yangon, attacked a Muslim man and destroyed the mosque he was attempting to protect after a dispute over its construction. Hundreds of other Muslim men and women have died in similar violent episodes in the Rakhine State. Hundreds of thousands of Muslims have fled the country. Sadly, violence between Muslims and Buddhists has been all too common since 2013. Surprisingly, some of those leading the violence are Buddhist monks.

There are reported to be over 500,000 monks and nuns (246,000 monks, over 300,000 novices, and about 45,000 nuns) in the Myanmar monastic community. Yet, while most of those monks are peaceful and compassionate Buddhist teachers, there are among them firebrand monks who regularly post hateful messages to their Facebook pages and preach nationalistic sermons of fear. Myanmar is at once a place of passion and meditation. Just as in all other religions, there are those who use and distort the tenants of the Buddhist religion for personal gain and or for the nationalistic exclusion of those they see as outsiders.

Hate, Nationalism, and Monks

In 2016 a radical monk, Ashin Wirathu, is infamous for his angry speeches that stoke fear. In speeches, sermons and social media, Wirathu claims that the Muslim minority is a security threat that will one day overrun the country. He is an ultranationalist who repeatedly speaks of the need to protect race and "protect Buddhism." Wirathu believes that he must protect Buddhism from Islam. His typical sermon begins: "Whatever you do, do it as a nationalist." In one sermon he said, "Muslims are like the African carp. They breed quickly and they are very violent and they eat their own kind. Even though they are minorities here, we are suffering under the burden they bring us." Some humans have a real talent for using religion to justify their own egos, needs, and fears. Obviously, Wirathu misunderstands metta, merit, and the basic tenants of his religion.

I planned to interview Wirathu to explore his thoughts on the relationship between the powers of government and religion. I wanted to know how he felt about the extremely close relationship between the dominant religion and the power of the Myanmar government. Again, the two institutions are very close, intertwined, and codependent. As a former political prisoner (Wirathu was sentenced to 25 years in prison in 2003 but was released in 2010 along with many other political prisoners), I thought he might have some interesting insights to share on that relationship. I was set to meet with this radical monk on a Wednesday afternoon in May in Mandalay. In preparation for my travel from Yangon to Mandalay (a one-hour flight) I stopped by the US Embassy cashier for a bit of traveling kyat. While standing at the window waiting for the cashier, one of the Embassy officials that coordinates the Fulbright scholars just happened to walk by and asked how I was doing. In my anticipation about my upcoming interview, I told her about my trip to Mandalay to meet with the infamous monk. Her facial expression changed quickly from calm to serious with concern when I shared my news. She quickly explained that she would have to check with the Ambassador and would get back with me. Then she added, "only the Ambassador has met with him, none of us are permitted to meet with him." I thought, why can't I keep my mouth shut? The next day I received this email. "Dear Bob, I checked in with [name omitted] and we would ask that you refrain from meeting with U Wirathu. There is a lot of risk of him playing up the engagement, especially since you are funded by the U.S. Government, and particularly after the demonstration last week. Sorry this throws a wrench in your plans, but I'm happy to discuss further if you have any questions." I canceled the interview.

The Muslim minority in Myanmar is suffering. Most (80%) of Myanmar's Muslim population live in Rakhine state. They call themselves the "Rohingya" people, and are Indo-Aryan peoples who speak the Rohingya language. They migrated to Myanmar from Bangladesh, during the period of British rule in Burma primarily between from 1824 to 1948. While it is obvious that they have lived in Myanmar for generations, the one million Rohingya are widely considered by Myanmar nationalists like Wirathu to be "illegal Bengalis' from neighboring Bangladesh. In recent years, hundreds of thousands of Rohingya have been stripped of official documentation, rendering them stateless. They face severe discrimination, must carry government issued identification cards indicating that they are Muslim, are restricted in travel, and must obtain official permission to marry. Several of my students identify as Rohingya. One Muslim student came to me after class and told me that he and his wife were having citizenship trouble with their one-year old daughter. He explained that both he and his wife held citizenship cards (all Myanmar citizenship cards include a person's ethnic identity and religion). The student, his wife, and their families had all been Myanmar citizens for several generations, but the Myanmar government refused to grant their one-year-old daughter a card or citizenship status. Of course, he is worried about his family, her life, and being able to continue living in Myanmar. He did not know where to go or what to do; I referred him to a group of Muslim lawyers. As I taught and delivered public lectures about basic human rights, tolerance, and an open society, many people would come up to me afterward and share such stories.

Steps with Metta

Obviously, violence against people of the Muslim faith is incongruent with the Buddhist philosophy of metta. To make this point and seek to change, several of my students recently organized a march in downtown Yangon titled "Steps with metta." The students were seeking to apply the practice of metta to the problems facing the Muslim people of Myanmar. In keeping with the long tradition of supporting one religion over another, the local government authorities interfered with the march, several groups tried to block the path of those marching, and later government officials charged the students for marching along what they later deemed was an unapproved route. At this writing the charges are still pending. The students and I are hoping that the new government is indeed reshaping the long held policy of supporting Buddhism and regulating religion. The next steps for the government to take are to follow my student's example and take steps with metta to treat all humans – regardless of their beliefs or backgrounds – with respect, compassion, and kindness. I do not imply that all, or even most, of Myanmar's monks are hateful nationalists, that is simply not the case.

A Monk's Life

In Myanmar today, there is a very large group of benevolent, peaceful, and very passionate politically active monks. Alison and I interviewed many of these monks, called "saffron monks," who took part in and or led the 2007 "saffron revolution" (an uprising against Myanmar's military government). I asked my students to share with me their favorite "monk story." Born in 1996 or so, my students well remember the saffron revolution. One student wrote, "When I was a child, I was surprised one day to see monks demonstrating with signboards. I was coming home from school and asked my mother, 'what is it?' She replied, 'People respect monks, so the monks are demanding the changes that the people need.'"

Another student wrote, "When I was young, I encountered the Saffron Revolution. I will never forget that many monks participated, many were arrested, and many were killed." Today the saffron monks loudly and strongly reject Wirathu, his followers, and their hateful and intolerant messages. The vast majority of the monks I interviewed were not at all hateful or intolerant. They were peaceful men who practiced metta. My interviews were arranged by my Myanmar friends and by the US Embassy. The monks were mostly very open (often they asked not to be named in my research as they still fear imprisonment) and they were almost all willing to discuss their beliefs (both political and religious) with me.

Myanmar's monks have for centuries played a central and critical role in nearly every aspect of the social and political life of the country. There is a very close daily relationship between the clergy and the people. The people provide for the monastic community and since the very earliest days (1044), monks have been the teachers of the people of Myanmar. Teachers are revered in Myanmar culture. Not only are they teachers of religion but also of secular learning (more on this in chapter six). Monks are typically well respected and are often looked to for advice and guidance. Monks of a local monastery will mediate a domestic dispute, scold an ungrateful teenager, or an unjust father. Many monks will point out an unjust government policy and often vocally advocate for basic human rights. They are very active with such statements on Facebook.

Monastery life is austere and disciplined, but also a

happy and cheerful endeavor. The monastery near our apartment sometimes sounded like a primary school yard with lots of laughter. The day begins very early, at dawn, with washing, chants, prayers, and a breakfast. After breakfast, alms-bowls are washed, and the monks attend a morning service and meditate. At about 9:00 in the morning all the monks and novices set out in a procession into the village for alms. They chat and laugh with one another as they walk in small groups of three or six. At 11:00 am or so (always before noon), they will eat their lunch. They will not eat again until breakfast the following morning. After an afternoon rest, the novices attend classes taught by older monks.

In the late afternoon at the Shwedagon Pagoda, for example, there is a good chance that one might strike up a conversation with a monk (in English) or quietly watch another play an intense game of chess with one of his students. The Shwedagon Pagoda, in Yangon, is one of the most famous pagodas in the world and is certainly the main attraction of all of Myanmar.

Myanmar monks today tell the story of how, in ancient times, two Mon merchant brothers traveled to pay homage to the Buddha, not long after the Buddha's enlightenment. The brothers are said to have obtained eight strands of the Buddha's hair (it's not clear how this happened and when I asked for those details of the stories the monks only laughed). They took those strands of the Buddha's hair back to Myanmar and gave them to their King (Okalappa) who had them enshrined in Shwedagon Pagoda. Today, the Shwedagon Pagoda is a beautiful, central, and revered place of worship and a symbol of both the Buddhist religion and the country. Many monks and nuns maintain the pagoda and grounds. One afternoon at the Shwedagon Pagoda, I happened upon a monk whose focus demonstrated the second stage of the path to enlightenment.

A Moment with Monk with a Cigar

The Buddha was not a god. He did not claim to be a god nor a savior. He simply wanted to be remembered as the one who woke up. After his enlightenment, the Buddha spent his life sharing his path to that waking or enlightenment. In fact, the Buddha had specific ideas and even techniques for achieving enlightenment. The Path he described is comprised of three stages: 1) morality (observance of the above Five Precepts); 2) meditation (achieving tranquility and insight); and 3) achieving wisdom (through tranquility and insight one obtains wisdom). In the meditation stage a person seeks a calm presence over the wandering and restless mind. One Cambodian nun said to me, "the mind travels, if it is not controlled. It is very difficult to control the mind, but one must control it in order to be tranquil."

Meditation allows one to achieve complete concentration on whatever one is doing, to the exclusion of all other stimuli. One of my students shared this story about meditation. These are his exact words, "Maybe it happened over last ten years. At this time, I went to the meditation center with my mother. I was too young among the adults (I was in grade 3 student). This meditation center was located in my village. Many people meditate, including me. It was in the afternoon, after having lunch. So, I was sleepy while meditating. The head monk saw me that I was sleeping and he shouted at me to wake up."

A variation of meditation is mindfulness. In a state of mindfulness, one attends exclusively to the present moment and becomes aware of his or her existence in that moment. Anyone can do this. Waking up does not take years of meditation in a Myanmar monastery. It only takes practice – the practice of living one's life recognizing that single moment actually matters. This moment is really all that there is; any moment in which you are unaware is lost. Many people live their entire lives unaware. I met a monk with a cigar who demonstrated mindfulness.

Alison Johnson Sterken meditates at the Shwedgaon Pagoda (2015).
Photo credit Robert Sterken.

On afternoon Alison was shopping for Buddha icons to take back to her yogi friends. I was just tagging along as she made her way along the many vendors lining the street toward the Shwedagon Pagoda. About half way up the street I noticed him. Sitting off to one side between two vendors, on a small plastic chair in a loosely tied saffron robe, was a monk with a cigar in his mouth at a rakish angle. His eyes were focused intently on the pieces on the chess board between him and a young man seated across from him. From a little distance away, I watched them play for a while.

There was something oddly fascinating about this monk. He was intensely focused. While there is debate about whether it is appropriate for monks to smoke or not, that was not the object of my fascination. I asked Alison to take his photo. She decided to ask him if it was okay before just snapping a picture. He waved her off, in English, saying that she was breaking his concentration, she was "interrupting his game." In that moment, I realized what it was that was so fascinating about the monk with the cigar and intense attitude. That monk was fully engaged in living in that very moment or so it seemed to me anyway. Relaxed, but focused on his chess pieces, with cigar in mouth he was awake, aware, and alive in that very moment.

None of us are immortal, and too often we deprive ourselves of the pleasure of this moment by worrying about the past or the future or a myriad of other travels of the mind. This monk, with no words, seemed to be saying that the moment must be embraced, this moment – this very moment. There he sat, a cigar-smoking, chess-playing monk engaged in his life. We are not lost because we are mortal and must ultimately die, instead, we are lost if we never actually live. It was a pleasure to meet, interview, and to just observe so many Myanmar monks, nuns, and novices. I remain ever grateful. Those interviews and many other experiences allowed me to know, confront, and even dismiss personal biases and prejudices.

Monk with cigar (2016). Photo credit: Alison Johnson Sterken.

Chapter 5

Race and Ethnicity: Meeting Myself

◊

Race and Reality

People look at me with suspicion when I try to explain how I met my own prejudice and saw the fibers of my own biases in Southeast Asia. Admitting that one has biases and prejudice makes one vulnerable. The entire conversation about race, ethnicity, and prejudices is too often fraught with emotion, awkwardness, and defensiveness. The subject is a minefield that many people simply refuse to enter. A friend of mine recently posted a well-meaning blog that listed twenty-eight common racist attitudes and behaviors that indicate a wrong turn, white guilt, denial, or defensiveness. The author followed each statement with his own "reality check and consequences" for such attitudes. While the blog post is helpful in pointing out racist attitudes, it also has the tone of and carries a hint of cultural insensitivity.

I see this all the time in my American classroom discussions about race. The students' families, cultures, and backgrounds have taught them to see the world in one way, but in the examination of those lessons they step into the minefield of twenty-eight racist attitudes. When they begin to talk openly, they too often find themselves in the awkward and uncomfortable position of not knowing what to say or where to step in a potentially hostile and emotional environment. The next step for too many is to retreat into withdrawal and silence. Interestingly, I witnessed almost the same silence, issues, and sensitive environment in my Myanmar classrooms.

Travel and Bigotry

In Myanmar, I met myself. Mark Twain was absolutely correct about the impact of travel. Twain wrote, "Travel is fatal to prejudice, bigotry, and narrow-mindedness, and many of our people need it sorely on these accounts. Broad, wholesome, charitable views of men and things cannot be acquired by vegetating in one little corner of the earth all one's lifetime." What sociologists call "intergroup contact" is one of the most powerful methods of exposing and reducing prejudice. Simply interacting with diverse groups of people often destroys prejudice, bigotry, and opens horizons. It's amazing to watch and even more amazing to experience. I highly recommend it.

You may be the most global of citizens and still find opportunities to challenge your prejudices. I did in Myanmar. Travel junkies are booking flights to Myanmar just so that they can see the beauty and mystery of an isolated and underdeveloped country and engage with a people far beyond their typical comfort zones. Even the most open and accepting of us has been taught to see the world in certain ways.

Seeing with new eyes is a beautiful gift. As a matter of routine, we all develop prejudices. We are far better humans if we routinely challenge those prejudices. Opening a book, traveling, trying a new point-of-view is not only healthy, but is also liberating.

It is a thrill to all of a sudden see something in a way that you have never seen before, but it can also be uncomfortable and challenging. Many people resist challenges to their current understanding of the world. Challenges to one's prejudice often means facing one's fear of the unknown and the possibility of change. People are also afraid of appearing to hold prejudices. Many people are afraid to admit ignorance of other cultures and other points-of-view. Attempting to be culturally sensitive is difficult, discomforting, and awkward, especially when ones does not know the subtleties of the culture. We do not want to be insensitive, clumsy, or ignorant, so we often fail to expose our prejudices and uninformed points-of-view to the needed light. I felt very clumsy and awkward when attending one very special event in Bangkok, Thailand.

On July 26, 2016, I gave a lecture at the United States Embassy in Bangkok. The lecture was the keynote event for a day-long official visit from Her Royal Highness Princess Sirindhorn and a group of military cadets from the Thailand Chulachomklao Royal Military Academy. The US Embassy had asked me to give the presentation to the Princess about seven months earlier. I had earlier given eight lectures for the United States Thai Embassy on democracy, an open society, and human rights at seven Thai universities and one with Ambassador Glyn Davies at the Embassy in Bangkok. For the event with the Princess, I arrived in Bangkok two days early to be briefed on the political nuances, review the content of my lecture, and then to rehearse for the event. It was during the rehearsal that I began to feel nervous, awkward, and concerned about culture and worried about doing and saying the right thing. I was given specific instructions on where to stand, how to hold my hands, how to bow, and what to say and how to say it. As the list of things grew, I worried that I would make some faux pas. Would I make a blunder in etiquette?

In my presentations, I often get very excited about sharing information and I was worried that I might slip and make an embarrassing blunder or forget to monitor my attitude about repressive military regimes. Fortunately, the day went off without a cultural hitch (as far as I know). I spent considerable time with the Princess (she went out of her way to talk with me) and answered lots of her questions as best I could. Princess Sirindhorn holds a PhD in History, so her questions were quite considered and thoughtful. One of the cadets was selected by his peers to thank me for the lecture. In perfect English he thanked me calling me, "His Excellency Dr. Robert Edward Sterken."

Over a lunch of snow fish prepared by Top Chef All Stars winner Richard Blais, the Princess asked me about Myanmar and my Yangon University students. Acknowledging the unknown culture and treating it with openness and honesty helped me be more at ease in the situation. I believe that I bowed correctly when the Princess gave me a gift.

We must realize that it is not a crime or sin to not know about other cultures and people or even to be ignorant of our own prejudices. It's okay not to know. It's important to embrace the fact that we are ignorant. We can learn! If we are able to recognize that we do not know, then we are poised to learn the new. We can discover our prejudices, privileges, and biases. We must embrace and seek experiences that challenge and bring light to our ignorance and destroy our prejudices.

The real shortcoming is to live in fear of learning, avoiding those challenges and checks to our world views. To refuse to learn and grow is to refuse to live a full life. To act upon one's evil prejudices and with ignorant narrow mindedness is the true sin. Too often humans do just that, act with bigotry born from the fears created by their ignorance and prejudices. Often humans even put those prejudices into law. I think that most people want to be open minded and most attempt to see beyond their socially constructed world views.

As I walked the streets in Yangon, I felt the joy of the changes and challenges to my perceptions of the world. My year of immersion in Burma allowed me to see myself more clearly than ever before. Living well beyond the normal confines of my American life allowed for a clear look at my soul. Being in Myanmar allowed me to see the underside of the world as if I was able to see the raw cogs, gears, and inner-workings of the clockwork of life in ways I had never seen before. The superficial was stripped away and I saw myself and others through unfiltered lenses.

Perhaps it was the Myanmar people who gave me this gift as they did not know the confines of my previous life and they appeared to me to be quite unpretentious. Myanmar life seemed more simple and to be unaffected. It could, in part, be their outward dress and appearance. Standing in traditional Western suits one evening in Mandalay, before I gave a lecture to Members of Parliament, a Senior US State Department official remarked, "It is hard for me to take any of this seriously when I'm standing here barefooted in a suit and tie." While there are beautiful traditional Myanmar dresses and a there is a formal attire for men, the clothing for everyday life for many Myanmar people often includes a wild mix-match colors and patterns. This down-to-earth style includes many people wearing a mud-like paste on their faces.

Thanaka

The women and children (and some men) of Myanmar wear "thanaka" mostly on their faces, but sometimes also on other exposed skin. Working in the rice fields under the tropical sun requires one to protect the skin. Seeing thanaka painted on a person's face for the first time is glimpse into the life of humans of another tribe. Engaging with another human tribe stretches one's mind in a way that it never goes back. Even little things, like learning about thanaka create an opportunity for intercultural understanding. When people in the United States flipped through my Facebook photos of Myanmar, one of the first thing they ask is about the coating of the yellowish white substance on the faces of the women and children. What is that on their faces? What is that for? The white substance is a cosmetic paste (it's makeup) made from ground bark. It has been a distinctive feature of the culture of Myanmar for over two-thousand years. It has a fragrant scent and is commonly applied in a circular patch on the cheeks, forehead, and nose. Thanaka is not only for cosmetic beauty, but it also cools the skin and protects it from the harsh tropical sun (there is debate about how effectively it protects the skin). Seeing thanaka somehow changes us. Likewise, my interactions with the people of Myanmar gave them contact with a person from another culture. We shared a curiosity about each other, we smiled across our differences, and in doing so learned a bit about ourselves.

Due to long-term lack of municipal infrastructure, many of the streets in Yangon are dirty. Too often they are stained red with Betel spit, littered with smashed plastic bottles, abandoned sandals, feral dog feces, oil, and garbage. I don't want to paint a dismal image of all Yangon streets, but the sad truth is that sanitation is not yet a strength of the Yangon municipality. It is, however, something that many local leaders are focused on, as in 2016 there are official public initiatives to clean up the city. Also, street lights are few and far between, so at night the streets are dark.

There are a few areas where the streets are well cleaned and well lit. However, walking down many streets at night is a far different experience than say walking in Chicago or San Diego or even Tyler, Texas at night. My first experiences with these streets, smells, and life were difficult. Difficult in that I felt insecure. If I found myself walking down such a street in London or Atlanta, I would be really worried. After a while, however, of walking the streets in Yangon, I felt a change. I could feel myself reconsider and confront my preconceived notions about street life, the conditions of the streets, and my own safety. We are taught lessons of what and who to fear and why. The streets of Yangon forced me to examine those lessons.

Crime rates (especially involving tourists) in Myanmar are very low. As a show of welcome, in 2013, the government established a "Tourist Police" unit to protect tourists against crime. In January 2015 to reinforce and strengthen that welcome, the government put up billboards directing Myanmar citizens to "warmly welcome foreigners" and to "take care" of them.

Rethinking Race

Living as a minority, in a place where it was rare to see someone with my fair skin color, allowed me to rethink "race." I felt what it is like to standout as "different." I have lived within the privileged status of a white male in the United States all my life. Again, this was not a status I chose or earned. In Yangon, I was suddenly and starkly the in minority. I was the really strange and tall foreigner. The new point-of-view gave me the gift of seeing how the concept of "race," both institutionally and socially, encompasses all too real advantages and disadvantages. Of course, I "knew" this intellectually, I had been teaching it for years, but in the streets of

Yangon I *felt* it.

The street life, the day-to-day living within a tribe so different from my own, and my daily work in Myanmar prompted an internal awakening to an another perspective on "race." I came to feel and see race differently. I came to better understand that we humans are not so different and even that the Myanmar people are my people – my brothers and sisters. One afternoon after giving a lecture at a university in northern Thailand, two graduate students came up to the front of the lecture hall to visit with me. They explained that they were from Myanmar and were excited that I was too. In an odd way, this tall Texan felt a kinship with those two students. The three of us, including me, were Myanmar people and we posed for photos.

Too often and sadly, race determines how we relate to one another. We humans do not live in "color blind" societies. Like most humans, the people of Myanmar struggle mightily with the issues of race and ethnicity. Every semester in my courses, I leap into a race and ethnicity conversation. I do this in the United States and I did it in Myanmar. It was a difficult subject for my Myanmar students, just as it is difficult for my students in the United States. It is always a challenge and it is frequently awkward, but I do it anyway. I believe that the artificial separation or classification of people into "races" to be one of humanities greatest and most wicked problems. Race is a wicked problem in that humans believe that they understand it, that it is common sense, and very often use it for evil. That is the case in the United States, Myanmar, and in far too many other places around the world. Myanmar's history, at least in part, is fraught with racial violence and ethnic conflict.

Every guidebook, every history book, and nearly every travel blog written about Myanmar covers race and ethnicity. The people of Myanmar practice many different cultural habits and rituals. Myanmar is by far the most diverse country in all of Asia, with no less than 135 separate cultures and many different languages, all living within an area about the size of Texas. Ethnologists find that all of these seemingly separate ethnic groups actually have their origins in just four groups who migrated to Burma: Tibeto-Burman, Mon-Khmer, Austro-Tai, and the Karennic.

Because of the lengthy interludes at traffic lights in Yangon, Mandalay, and elsewhere, vendors line the streets to sell large laminated ethnolinguistic maps of the country. I have never been in a country where large maps of ethnic peoples were regularly sold at busy street intersections (along with bottles of water, betel, calendars, and photos of Aung San Suu Kyi). It is often hard for the vendor to carry the large slippery maps as he attempts to show and sell them to people in taxis. When I moved into my Hledan apartment there was one taped to the wall in the living room. Whenever I met a new Myanmar person, almost without exception, one of the very early details he or she shared would be ethnic identity. "Hi, I am Htuk Htuk, I am Karen." Taxi drivers would say, "I am Rakhine." One of my students proudly announced, "I am Mon." Like a proud Texan, students of mine wore t-shirts declaring their tribe: "Proud Karen."

Today, the Myanmar people regularly use race/tribe/ethnicity as identity markers. Historians tell us that this was not always the case. In the pre-colonial days, ethnicity, race, and languages were not the fixed unipolar identities that they came to be under the British. Before the British, religion (Buddhist or not) and allegiance to the King were the primary identity markers. To administer the country, the British standardized, defined, named, and precisely mapped the territories and the people. In doing this they reified race and ethnicity and made those identity markers a social, legal, and political matter. Historians are careful not to lay all blame on the British, but the consensus is that in general, race and ethnic markers of identity were not commonly or self-consciously held in the pre-colonial days.

The British, later the Burmese military, and in 2015 the quasi-civilian government each defined in specific legal terms, the races or ethnic divisions in Myanmar. While some terms (for example Rohingya) are specifically prohibited for political reasons, it's important to understand that all of the terms or categories are social constructions. Creating categories of humans is fraught with problems and politics. There is a very real need to establish a better method of discussing cultural differences and understanding Burma's diversity.

In June 2016, the Tibetan spiritual leader, the Dalai Lama, urged Daw Aung San Suu Kyi to make efforts to reduce racial and ethnic tensions in Myanmar. In August 2016, Suu Kyi was engaged in significant reconciliation efforts to end the decades of fighting between the military and myriad rebel groups. Daw

Suu made an appeal to the Myanmar people to overcome their differences and to work together to achieve peace.

Many of my students are suffering and living under two stark "race" policy decisions made by the Myanmar government. First, in the 1960s, the military decided to create national identity cards in which a person's religion and race is recorded. Second, in 2015, the government passed four laws for "the protection of race and religion." Those two policies embalmed in Myanmar law the burdens of the prejudices of the Myanmar society. The laws not only reflect the prejudices, but have themselves become instruments in the construction and reinforcement of racial and religious conflict. The laws are the tools and the cause of division, discrimination, and often violence. The Myanmar leaders who drafted these laws thought that they understood race.

To Be Burmese is to be Buddhist

After the British and the Japanese left Burma, the leaders of the newly independent state sought to form or re-form a national identity. In the 1960s, and again in recent years, Burma saw the widespread emergence of ethnic nationalism or ethno-nationalism. Just as some in the United States argue should be done, many of the people of Burma sought to define their national identity in terms of their perceived ethnicity and religion. Rather than describe their country in terms of shared values, they sought to define it in terms of ethnic ancestry (which is horribly divisive). Very often during my year in Myanmar, I heard Myanmar people refer to themselves as "pure Burman." About forty million (of the total 55 million) Myanmar people identify as "Bamar" or Burman. This group, known as Burmans by the British, originally migrated from southern China, make up the country's dominate racial group.

With laws like the national identity card and the protections of race and religion, the government created cultural domination, racial oppression, and promoted strong and divisive identity markers. Under the slogan, "To Be Burmese is to be Buddhist," leaders intertwined race and ethnicity with religion and national identity. This ethno-nationalistic movement made it seem necessary to "protect the country's religion and race" from anyone not seen as part of the dominant group. Protecting a religion and race is a wicked practice that permeates Myanmar politics.

As I walked through the many widely diverse street-food vendors in the Hledan township of Yangon, people would often stop me and ask what country I call home. My fair skin and blue eyes marked me as racially different in their eyes, but they were unable to identify me as an American with German-French origins. They had to ask, in order to know, and they sometimes did. The people of Myanmar had not been taught the social mythologies often assigned to my family background. Nor had I been taught to know the markers for "race" of the people asking me questions. I could not mark a person from China or India, Shan state or Karen, or Rahkine, I was not taught those "race" markers. Race is obviously a social construction. We are taught to "see" race.

Because our training in "seeing" race starts very early and the concept that it is socially constructed is often difficult to grasp. We create artificial differences. Being vulnerable and frail humans, many people turn to race and religion for status and make sense of life.

I spent considerable amounts of my time in Myanmar giving public lectures about democracy, tolerance, diversity, and an open society. Very often I would address the issue of "race." You may be wondering why. Why even bring up the issue of race? My answer is backed by decades of research that tells us that not talking about race or avoiding the discussion does not make the issue go away. Research suggests that when parents do not talk about race with their children the children still notice it anyway, they take note of the silence, and the avoidance only leads to misunderstanding and ignorance. Not talking about race nurtures biases, bigotry, and surprisingly problematic views about the issue. Pretending to be "colorblind" and being "race-mute" does not lead us to understand racial issues, rather it amounts to willful ignorance. Racism is acceptable and a very routine part of nearly all people in Myanmar today. The Myanmar people do not pretend to be colorblind and they are far from color-mute. One Myanmar national with whom I regularly worked with in the US Embassy told me that the Rohingya were commonly called "kalar" and that they had dark skin and were not like the "fair and beautiful little Burmese people."

In my public lectures and classrooms, my statement that race is not biologically determined but socially constructed, was almost universally met with blank

stares of disbelief. I would say, "Scientists tell us that
we are all one people, all one species – we are just
humans. There are no genetic characteristics
possessed by all Burmans, that are not carried by non-
Burmans," and the audience would sit in motionless
silence. I would plow on, "Biologists tell us that a
person's race is not determined by a single gene or
even group of genes." Then pointing at my fair-
skinned arm I would say, "We are far more alike than
we are different." Into the silence I would then hear a
few nervous laughs when I asked if the interpreter
needed me to slow down. Yes, we can see very minor
differences in genetics, but those differences are a
function of separation, usually geographic, and occur
only very gradually across regions of the world,
rather than within precise lines. Since genetic
differences correlate to geography, not to notions of
race, there are no sharp divisions between the people
of Myanmar or even across the people of all of Asia.
Contrary to popular opinion, science refutes the
supposition that race reflects genetic differences (look
it up). Maya Angelou's poem "The Human Family"
makes this point.

The Human Family

I note the obvious differences
in the human family.
Some of us are serious,
some thrive on comedy.
Some declare their lives are lived
as true profundity,
and others claim they really live
the real reality.
The variety of our skin tones
can confuse, bemuse, delight,

brown and pink and beige and purple,
tan and blue and white.
I've sailed upon the seven seas
and stopped in every land,
I've seen the wonders of the world
not yet one common man.
I know ten thousand women
called Jane and Mary Jane,
but I've not seen any two
who really were the same.
Mirror twins are different
although their features jibe,
and lovers think quite different thoughts
while lying side by side.
We love and lose in China,
we weep on England's moors,
and laugh and moan in Guinea,
and thrive on Spanish shores.
We seek success in Finland,
are born and die in Maine.
In minor ways we differ,
in major we're the same.
I note the obvious differences
between each sort and type,
but we are more alike, my friends,
than we are unalike.
We are more alike, my friends,
than we are unalike.
We are more alike, my friends,
than we are unalike.
- Maya Angelou

This human-created race issue has placed the Myanmar Rohingya people in the untenable position of being born on this planet and not having a home. The Rohingya people are stateless. They have no claim to Bangladesh citizenship nor to the country in which they were born. Stop for a second and just imagine being stateless. A stateless person has no country to call home. Our definitions of race limits our ability to recognize that we are all just humans residing in a single skin, carrying our hopes, dreams, memories, and fears.

Race and Consequences

One of my most successful Myanmar students, the young man who was called horrible racist names as a child, showed me his National Identity Card during a class break one night. National ID cards are nearly always controversial. The first Myanmar National Identity Cards were issued in 1952, but only to certain parts of the country and to specific groups. In 1962, the military issued identity cards to all Myanmar citizens, expect monks. Monks were not issued identity cards until the 1980s. In the 1980s, Buddhist monks became a vocal and strong opponent to the Myanmar military government and the government sought to control the monastic community, in part by requiring them to be issued and hold ID cards to keep track of them. Until the 1980s, there were only two types of people in Myanmar, citizens and foreigners. A new citizenship law, in 1982, sorted people into various new racial and religious identities.

In recent years, some political leaders in the United States called for national identity cards and a registry system. Identity cards that define a person's ethnic, racial, or religion are understandably controversial and in Myanmar quite divisive. The card forces a person to be affiliated with a governmentally-defined group. One of my students told me that he was forced to identify as "Indian" even though he was born in Myanmar, as were several generations of his family. The Myanmar national identity card is used to discriminate and often leads to human rights abuses. Myanmar officials and others in the society use the card classifications to target people by government created identity markers.

The 2016 Myanmar National Identity card, requires each person to note both "race' and "religion." If a person is Buddhist, the card is commonly noted that their race is either "Bama" or one the seven major ethnic groups. But if a person is a practicing Muslim, the card must and will also note a "race" from one of three other countries: India, Bangladesh, or Pakistan. One of my students said, "There are some friends of mine who are purely "Bama" or "Mon" as race, but since they converted from Buddhism to Islam, they were forced to put those foreign races in their ID card. It doesn't make sense to them that they were pure ethic race when they were Buddhists, but all of a sudden become "Indian," "Bengali" or "Pakistani" once they converted to Islam. On my ID card it is written that I am Indian, Sunni (a Pakistani tribe name) although I was born here in Myanmar and have never been to those countries, never knew about those cultures, and never spoken or understood any of their languages. I am from Myanmar!"

The Rohingya (mostly people who hold the Muslim faith), suffer greatly under the identity card classifications of the 1982 Citizenship Law. They face severe restrictions on freedom of movement, access to health care, and are denied their basic rights to education and employment opportunities. Because of my oft repeated bold statements of support, Muslim students would come up to me after public lectures and classes and share their stories. One student said, "When registering for a national identity card, Myanmar immigration officers force Muslim residents to identify themselves as mixed blood of Indian and Burmese race." Myanmar residents normally apply for a card when they are ten years old and then get a new card when they turn eighteen. Another student said, "My friend is Mon, he got a card when he turned eighteen. His new card changed him to mixed blood. He is now Mon + India, because he is Muslim."

Without an official identity card and all of its designations, a person cannot graduate from any school and cannot travel. My Muslim students told me in unison one night that "if you are of mixed blood, you are a second class citizen." They told me that, "If your ID card says you are of mixed-blood, you cannot apply for a government job and the government schools allow only a few Muslim teachers." In my classes at Yangon University I had very few self-identified Muslim students. One student said, "Because I am mixed race Muslim, the process to get an ID card takes a very long time. As for me, it's now over two years and still in process."

The ID card leads to everyday discrimination. Another of my students said, "Once any immigration officer sees my ID card, he will realize that I am a Muslim. Even when I don't feel the need to tell others what religion I belong to as I think that religion is a private matter. Once the immigration officer sees that I am Muslim, they often say, 'You are a Muslim and you can't travel to this place.' So in order to get passed the checkpoint Muslims have to bribe officers." Another student wrote, "If When I am staying in a hotel, I have to show my ID card, and the reception or the hotel owner will see that I am a Muslim. If they are extreme Buddhist nationalists, a Muslims can feel really threatened and unsafe just even staying there. Sometimes they will not even allow us to stay."

Many Muslim students told me that the treatment they receive at the official immigration office was often the most difficult and expensive that they experienced. They all described having to bribe immigration officials (usually $200 USD) to even get a national identity card. One student reported, "Recently, I went to renew my passport at the immigration office in Yangon. After standing in one line, I realized that I can't line up in the same line with Buddhist people. They make Muslims (also some Chinese and Christians) line up in a separate line which leads to the office of the head of immigration office. Muslims have to queue in a separate line and pay bribe to get their passports. We had to meet with the head of the immigration office one-on-one. The head officer would find any possible reasons to get bribes from non-Buddhists. I refused to bribe."

Two of my students, Mr. Aung Kaung Myat (from Buddhist family) and Mr. Than Toe Aung (from Muslim family), wrote and recited in tandem their poem "It starts with you" at a Poetry Slam in August of 2016 in Yangon. The poem was very widely shared in social media and on print media.

It starts with you

When I was young,
A dark-skinned Indian-looking kid sat next to me in the
class Because nobody wanted to sit with him
The moment I got home, I asked my parents "why?"
When I was young,
I knew my teacher hated me
She never treated me well and looked me with disgust So I
asked my parents "Why?"
My parents said, "Son, he is not like us." "They are
Kalars"
My parents said, "Don't mind it. Just focus on your
studies" But the question still lingers in my heart
"Why?" Is it because we are Muslims? It is because they
are Muslims They are subject to all the mistreatment and
discrimination Is it right for us to live like nothing is
wrong in this society?
With the Government ID explicitly saying what your
religion is
With the school textbooks that constantly tell the children
throughout their school
How Burmese were a great race and how Buddhism is a
great religion
With the government's official list of 135 ethnic races
where the Chinese and Indians are deliberately left out
With the national identity focusing on religion and religion
alone With the mob attacks and riots happening here and
there
As a kid, I have this question, why?
Why people look my friend in a weird way
Why my teacher did not show any kindness and affection
towards me Like she did to my classmates
So, tonight I will tell you
I will tell you what their pretty labels
"host"
"guest"

Changed the way people think
I will tell you how racism has been going on in Burma for decades but no one including politicians cares to change it
I will tell you how it feels like to live with fear when nationalists threaten to burn down your house and kill your family
I will tell you, no one ever asked to be born in a Buddhist or Muslim family I will tell you how you'll find out there is no such thing as a pure race if you have a DNA test
So, what is it like to be a Buddhist in Burma?
It means nothing except that you can sell stuff at the pagodas ... without troubles Unlike that Muslim vendor who was beaten and held against his will
By a group of monks
It means nothing except that you can go anywhere
Unlike a group of Muslims in Rakhine state who can't move an inch out of the concentration camps
It means nothing except that your attendance to Ethnic Youth Conference Will never be denied
It means nothing except that a group of thugs will never set your house on fire For a religion you practice
When you physically attack someone because of his religion You don't attack him, you attack the freedom of worship Which is guaranteed by the Constitution
You don't attack him, you attack the beauty of diversity That holds us together as a society
You don't attack him, you attack the fundamental principles of democracy
Let us all be united against racism
Let us all tell them there is no place for racism in our civilized society It must start now and it starts with you

~ by Aung Kaung Myat & Than Toe Aung

Protection of Race and Religion

In 2015, the Myanmar military controlled parliament passed a set of "Protection of Race and Religion" laws, which impose restrictions on religious conversion, interfaith marriage, and even childbirth. They stipulate who can convert to a different faith, and grant government officials and community members power to "approve" applications for conversion. The laws also exclusively target and regulate the marriage of Buddhist women with men from another religion. The legal codification of race has created a wicked problem in Myanmar. US Supreme Court Justice Thurgood Marshall said it best, "Racism separates but it never liberates. Hatred generates fear, and fear once given a foothold, binds, consumes and imprisons. Nothing is gained from prejudice. No one benefits from racism."

The Thomas theorem of sociology applies perfectly to the "race" conflict and wicked problem facing the people of Myanmar; "If men define situations as real, they are real in their consequences." What "race" you are in the Myanmar obviously has enormous social, economic, and political consequences. Those consequences are real and affect the people, regardless of whether "race" is real or not. The government of Myanmar has defined "race" as real. The consequences of those real-world identity markers are overt and ugly discrimination, divisiveness, othering, intolerance, and all too often even violence. In the everyday lives, people in shops, neighborhoods, and even in their celebrations, are far more alike than their identity cards indicate. For example, the Myanmar people – all of the people

(Buddhists, Muslims, Christians) – all across the country celebrate Thingyan. Imagine Christmas, New Year, or Super Bowl day in the United States, and then imagine all of the stores and shops are closed – none remain open, not even Walgreens. Then take it one step further, everyone celebrates not just for the one day but for four (and in some years five) days! Unlike many expats, I stayed in Myanmar during the five days Thingyan.

Thingyan: A Washing Away

It gets really hot in Myanmar in April. Being from Texas, I have known heat. But the Myanmar heat is different. It feels so much hotter because the rays of the sun shine from directly – or nearly directly – overhead. During the hot months, March, April and May, the sun shines directly on the equator and the Myanmar people and dogs all desert the streets for shade during the peak sun hours of the day. I took an extra shirt to almost all destinations during those months. The streets come to life again at around six each evening. But during the four days of Thingyan they are teeming with merry making all day long. Thingyan, held annually in mid-April, is the Burmese New Year. Although it is a Buddhist water festival, all people in Myanmar, it seems without exception, celebrate over the four to five days that culminates in their New Year.

People spray, throw water, and sprigs of thabyay on everyone walking by. Everyone is fair game except monks, nuns, and pregnant women. I got very wet. It seems that the tall foreigner was a delightful target. Children are told that if they have been good, then

Thagya Min will take their names down in a golden book, but if they have been naughty their names will go into a dog book.

The water is a symbolic baptism, intended to wash away the heat and sins of the previous year. Garden hoses, syringes made of bamboo, brass or plastic, water pistols, and other devices from which water can be squirted are used in addition to the gentler bowls and cups. Water balloons and even fire hoses are also routinely used. It is the hottest time of the year, so a good dousing is welcome – by most.

Thingyan allowed me and all of the Myanmar people to celebrate together. To throw water on one another allowed each of us to see the other as an individual. I like to think that celebrating together, allowed us to override our pre-existing biases. My own interactions in the wet streets, shaking hands with young and sometimes very drunk men and being soaked from behind by strangers and children, allowed me to see the beautiful people of Myanmar as unique individuals. Being doused with buckets of ice water, in a friendly manner, somehow christened me as one of them. I had traveled half way around the world, to a land like no other, only to find that we are really far more alike than we are different. I felt the water of Thingyan wash away some of our differences and somehow even initiate me into the culture. The acceptance validated my global citizen identity card. Perhaps this is only wishful thinking on my part, but then if a man defines a situation as real in his own mind, it becomes real in its consequences.

Chapter 6

Teaching Barefoot: The Earth as My Witness

◊

The U Chit Tea Shop

The trouble began at the U Chit Tea Shop. Or at least that how the authorities saw it – as trouble. The students and professors saw it as the beginning of a revolution – and each time, it was. The trouble (or revolution) started at the U Chit Tea Shop in the 1920s and 1930s, again in the 1960s, again in the 1980s, and yet again in 1990s. There was almost always something brewing at the U Chit Tea Shop. After one of my first classes at Yangon University, a small group of students approached me and asked me to join them for tea. As we sat down at the plastic tables in red plastic chairs under an umbrella I was unaware of the rich history of the famous gathering spot for Yangon University students. Teaching political science to Myanmar students was an education unlike any I have ever experienced. While I was sharing concepts, research, ideas, and data, I was learning in profound and new ways about the realities of unchecked power, undying optimism, and most of all, the beauty and power and gift of higher education.

An acquaintance of mine who lives in Tyler, Texas rhetorically asked on my Facebook wall, "What is the purpose of higher education; other than just a breeding ground for malcontents?" Too often people see the unrest of professors and students as a threat to the norms and status quo of society. Education offers the learner the opportunity to not only lead a productive life, but also to become aware. Becoming aware, waking up, is indeed empowering. Realizing that life does not have to be the way that it has always been, often means challenging the status quo. At the U Chit Tea Shop, students and professors have regularly gathered after classes for generations to discuss politics and history. I had the pleasure of doing just that with my students and a few faculty members on several occasions. At different points in the history of Burma, the intellectual debates at the U Chit tea shop grew into rallies and even nationwide protests. The "malcontents" demanded change.

My Myanmar Students

The US Embassy assigned me a heavy teaching load. In my year in Myanmar, I taught eight courses at three different institutions. I taught three courses (two undergraduate level and one graduate level) in the College of Liberal Arts at Myanmar Institute of Theology (MIT), two courses (both graduate level) at the Yangon School of Political Science, and three courses (two graduate level and one honors undergraduate course) at Yangon University. It was intense, demanding, but rewarding work. The classrooms were not air-conditioned and the tropical heat made teaching a real workout. My students often worried about me when my shirt was drenched and sweat dripped from my glasses. My body never really adjusted to the strain and intensity of the heat, even after teaching in the hot and humid conditions for a year; I was drenched and completely exhausted after each class. I would return to the apartment thoroughly exhausted and depleted and would often be too tired to cook and thus lost a significant amount of weight.

Teaching Myanmar students was an extraordinary experience. All (or nearly all) of my Myanmar students were unbelievably motivated. Just walking into a classroom filled with Myanmar students was inspiring. While they were not well prepared for the demands of a college course, they made up for it with rapt attention, hard work, and enthusiasm. Class attendance was nearly always at one hundred percent (or even greater as several students attended who were not on the rolls). Doing well was of utmost importance for nearly all of my Myanmar students. For the 200 seats in the 2016 Freshman class in the MIT Liberal Arts program, the college received more than 2500 applications.

Myanmar college students were different from my American students in three ways. First, the Myanmar students (both men and women) dressed well to attend each and every class. Both sexes wore the longyi every day, no shorts were worn in any of my classes. Men always wore collared shirts and women wore traditional skirts, typically paired with lace or satin blouses. Second, while there is respect for professors in the United States, professors in Myanmar are deeply revered. As I said earlier this was not easy to handle. Third, and related to the respect, the Myanmar students were extremely reluctant to answer the questions I posed in class.

Arr-Nar-Tel

My students would just look blankly at me when I asked them questions. Then, if I waited long enough, they would become embarrassed and look down at their desks. Not once in the entire year, was I challenged on a point made in class. Other professors told me that Myanmar K12 students are not taught to think critically, but instead are taught to be silent in the classroom and to never to ask questions. When I asked my students about this, they said "we feel backward, but backward isn't the right word." I pushed them to tell me more and they explained about the Myanmar concept of "arr-nar-tel." My students explained that the Myanmar words "arr-nar-tel" do not translate into English (which is in itself interesting). The phrase, in part, means that the Myanmar person does not want to make the other person uncomfortable. The Myanmar person does not want to cause any negative social tension toward the other person. Thus, my students would not answer my questions because they did not want to appear to make me do or say something that I did not want to do or say. At its foundation politics is about conflicts of values and principles, thus my subject is fraught with social tension. It is not that my Myanmar students were at all disinterested. Indeed, they were all listening, and but with the reverence they give to professors, coupled with arr-nar-tel, they just would or could not respond to my questions. By not responding they thought and felt that they were being considerate of my feelings. Even after I explained that my feelings would not be hurt and that it was my

Teaching Barefoot in Burma

desire and choice to be challenged and questioned, they still did not want to make me feel uncomfortable. They did not want me to feel challenged by them or to create any social tension. They also felt that the professor and student social boundary prohibited them from responding. Responding across that social boundary would cause them to feel guilty. One day one of my graduate students stood up next to his desk and asked a question. I thought that I was making some progress. With his voice shaking and with halting English he finally completed his statement. It turned out that he merely wanted me to repeat what I'd just said. I encouraged and modeled respectful challenges of ideas for my Myanmar students; I wanted them to think critically and to challenge authority. I would regularly challenge myself, or even pretend that one of the students had asked a challenging question. In the end, however, I found that the best way to encourage them to answer was to break them into small groups and allow them to debate the concept without me. Sometimes it's best to get off the stage. There were many times that my Myanmar students asked me to slow down. I tend to get very animated while teaching and I talk fast. I would apologize for my "bad English" and worked at speaking slowly and leaving a pause between each word, which is a challenge, especially during a long lecture. There were times when we just could not understand one another. My cultural background and language did not provide me with the tools to understand them initially, so I sat down with them and asked them to explain. Those conversations – when my students were teaching me – were very powerful. I assumed the role of the student and we became a community of bonded learners.

Education is changing Myanmar, but even with the new government in place, the opportunity to attend a university and to earn a degree was something still very rare in 2016. The story of Myanmar higher education is both tragic and prophetic. It is tragic in the sense that what was once great, is no longer. The higher education system was literally destroyed by the military. It is prophetic in that Americans and others around the world must take note of the consequences when government does not have faith in or support higher education. In a time when public (state) funding in public colleges and universities in the United States is being cut, the Myanmar story should serve as a warning of the dangers of governments that fail to properly support public higher education. In 1878, the British government decided to invest in higher education in Burma and created Rangoon College (later renamed Yangon University) as an affiliate of the University of Calcutta. Between the 1880s and 1930s, Yangon University grew to be one of the world's most prestigious institutions of higher education.

By the 1940s, Yangon University was widely regarded as one of the best universities in all of Asia and attracted students and faculty from around the world. The British modeled the institution after the Universities of Oxford and Cambridge and today the architecture still reflects that influence (albeit the buildings are now in great need of repair and renovation). From the turn of the century until the 1960s, with all courses taught in English, the University of Yangon offered professional degrees in liberal arts, law, medicine, sciences, and education. It was a world-class institution.

U Chit Tea Shop 1920s and 1930s

Every morning on my way to class, I passed a cornerstone on a Yangon University building that read: "This foundation stone was laid by his Excellency Sir Charles Innes, K.C.S.I., C.I.E., I.C.S., Governor of Burma, Chancellor of the University, the 3rd of November 1928." Mr. Innes' titles indicate that he was a Knight Commander of the Star of India (KCSI), a Companion of the Most Eminent Order of the Indian Empire (CIE), and a member of the Indian Civil Service (ICS). With his highly polished English shoes tied neatly to his feet, Sir Charles Innes oversaw a great deal of construction on the Yangon University campus, where he lived and worked from December 1927 to December 1932.

All the work in creating a world-class university paid off for Sir Charles Innes and the British government in a way that they probably did not expect. Education has a unique way of empowering learners. In the 1920s and 1930s those newly empowered college students formed the center of the anti-colonial movement. Meeting first at the U Chit Tea Shop the students began three nationwide strikes against the British colonial government (1920, 1936, and 1938).

By the late 1930s, the University's political science department was nurturing and supporting the growth of Burmese nationalism and the movement toward independence. In those years, Yangon University produced a number of future senior Burmese politicians, including General Aung San, the famous father of Aung San Suu Kyi. Aung San and several of his classmates eventually managed to break free of British colonial occupation. The student's protest of the British occupation started over shoes.

The Shoe Question

The British who ruled Burma from 1824 to 1948 were quite particular about their shoes and boots. With their shoes on, the British have been known to be uptight, reserved, even snobbish, and yet often treat others with a polite but cold detachment. In their boots, the British ruled Burma as an independently administered colony under the province of British India. The British influence on the people and the land of Burma is still very evident today, in part because little has changed since they left the colony to self-rule in 1948. As such a determined, disorganized, Burmese nationalism eventually developed. One of the early manifestations of this anti-colonial nationalism came to a boil over the uptight and rigidly conventional British "shoe question."

In 1916 a lawyer, U Thein Maung, visited the Shwe Sandaw Pagoda in Bagan. Built by the revered and legendary Burmese King Anawrahta in 1057, the Shew Sandaw Pagoda is one of the many and very sacred Buddhist pagodas in Myanmar. The British had placed a sign at the entrance of the pagoda that read, "No one is permitted to wear shoes in this Pagoda but Englishmen and Asiatic Europeans." U Thein Maung was incensed and pulled down the sign and had it replaced with another sign that banned footwear for all people who wished to visit the pagoda. The British authorities demanded that the new sign be removed and the old sign replaced. Rather than adhere to this demand and replace the sign, the Burmese nationalists installed the all-inclusive signs at all religious sites in the country. Tensions grew. The "shoe question" became a national political issue in Burma and the more radical nationalists formed a political organization to fight the shoe question and to push for Burmese independence. Shoes, it turned out, were a big deal.

U Chit Tea Shop 1962

One morning on my way to class, I was stopped on my street by a small, elderly, man walking slowly with a cane. He wore a dark longyi, a white western style sport coat, and wire rimmed glasses. The sport coat was an unusual article of clothing in Yangon. It was not uncommon for the Myanmar people to stop me. Often children would practice their English when I walked by, saying, "Helloooo, hooooww are youuu, tooodaaay?" in a sing-song fashion. I did not expect it at all, but the elderly man spoke to me in the most perfect British English. When he found out where I was teaching, he told me that he had graduated from Yangon University in 1956. "I was one of the last cohorts," he said, "to get a real education at that wonderful institution."

The military generals who took over the Burmese government in 1962, also took over the control of Yangon University. They put the university under the direct control of the military and immediately prohibited the study or use of the English language and specifically prohibited the study of political science. With academic freedom gone and funding cut, the quality of education so dramatically declined that international bodies stopped recognizing degrees granted by the University.

On the 7th of July 1962, to protest the "unjust university rules" and the decline of their university the students once again gathered at the U Chit Tea Shop. By the time troops arrived hundreds of students had gathered. The students refused to disperse. The military killed fifteen students and wounded many more. The very next morning, military trucks arrived at the historic University Student Union building (the building that housed the famous U Chit Tea Shop). The legendary building, an icon of student activism and protest was obliterated, literally blown to pieces by dynamite. In an attempt to quell student activism, the military expelled all of the foreign faculty, fired all of the foreign trained Burmese faculty, and divided up the administration of the university into several independent units. Students were murdered, professors were strictly controlled, and the institution was ripped apart, but the military could not destroy ideas or the unquenchable thirst for learning. The remaining faculty and a few students limped along under these strained conditions until 1988.

U Chit Tea Shop 1988

Khin Sandar was born in October 1988. Two months before her birth, Yangon University students once again initiated a series of protests that spread throughout the country. The Burmese military opened fire on the student protestors again, this time killing more than one thousand students. In July of 2016, I met Khin at the famous U Chit Tea Shop (now in a different location) on campus to discuss her research. Khin was my student at another institution, the Yangon School of Political Science (YSPS), and at my urging, she was writing about the impact of women in the Myanmar Parliament. After having coffee and talking about her work for a while, she looked around and said, "I've always loved it here." I did not know what she meant, the tea shop was rather ordinary and the campus was quite unkempt. The Yangon University landscape and buildings have not been cared for or maintained since the 1960s. One of my South Korean colleagues noted that his first impression in 2012 of the University was that "it is like an old, deserted palace." The jungle has all but reclaimed the once beautiful campus. Khin continued, "This place of learning, this campus has always been so special to me. Ever since I was a little girl, it was my dream to come to school here. But I never got the chance. The military closed the school and no one in my generation got to go. Few even got to go to college at all." The year Khin was born, the military closed the campus because of the government's fear of students like U Ko Ko Gyi.

In 1988, Ko Ko Gyi was in his final year of college. He was an international relations major in the department of international relations at Yangon University. He and his fellow classmates, including the current Chair of the International Relations Department, Dr. Chaw Chaw Sein, regularly gathered at the U Chit tea shop after classes to discuss and debate history, politics, and policy. In March 1988, at the start of the 88 Uprising, Ko Ko Gyi, together with his fellow students, led a peaceful march and rally. Starting at the tea shop on the campus, the students attempted to march a couple of miles down Insein Road to the Yangon Institute of Technology in support of the Yangon Tech students who had recently been beaten and shot by the military police.

As they marched off the campus, Ko Ko Gyi and his classmates were severely beaten by the military police on the main street in front of the University. Ko Ko Gyi was arrested and spent the next several months in jail. Upon his release the young political science student returned to his University only to once again rally and protest against the military government. On December 11th 1991, Ko Ko Gyi and his classmates organized another rally on the campus, this time to support and honor Aung San Suu Kyi, who was then under house arrest. Ko Ko Gyi was once again arrested and this time was sentenced to twenty years in the Insein Prison with hard labor. The government closed all schools in the country for two years. After spending the next thirteen years in prison Ko Ko Gyi was released in March 2005. No longer a young political science student, but still a fighter for justice and democracy, he immediately resumed his fight against the unjust and inhumane actions of the military government.

In September 2006, Ko Ko Gyi was again arrested for his overt pro-democracy activities and spent the next several years in prison. In January 2012, he was finally released from prison when he and nearly six hundred other political prisoners were pardoned by the quasi-civilian government. Ko Ko Gyi, now in his mid-fifties, has spent over seventeen years of his life in prison in response to his relentless stand for basic human rights and democracy. Today, Ko Ko Gyi is a vocal and outspoken advocate for human rights and social justice, a role that was not possible until November 8, 2015.

Like my acquaintance in Texas, the Burmese military generals saw Yangon University as a breeding ground for malcontents. After the 88 uprising the military closed all schools in the country for a year and Yangon University for two years. After two years, the University was reopened, but only to graduate students. The institutions funding was dramatically cut, and students were not allowed to study political science or history. The Yangon University political science department was closed and remains so still in 2016.

In October 1996, yet another student uprising took place. This time the military shuttered all higher education opportunities in the country (except distance education) until 2013. It was not until March of 2011 that the military government led by President U Thein Sein began to shake off the decades of isolation and to take steps toward becoming an open and internationally engaged society. As part of that effort the government reopened Yangon University in 2013. The undergraduate honors students I taught in 2016 were the first class of students to study at the University since 1996. On behalf of Khin and a few others, I asked the Yangon University administration to grant permission for my YSPS students to sit in on my lectures. The reply was telling. After hesitating, the administrator said, "Yes, it's okay, as long as they do not start a protest." The administrator knew that my YSPS students were exactly the type who just might gather at the U Chit Tea Shop.

The Yangon School of Political Science

The semester I taught at YSPS gave me a new understanding of the discipline of political science and framed my teaching in a new light. It added urgency to my work. It made me want to tell you this story. The Yangon School of Political Science is unlike any other political science program in the world. It is a young institution, founded in 2011. The US Embassy in Yangon initiated my connection with the institution and I taught in the school for a complete semester. I did not think that I was in the right place when my taxi stopped at the address of the school on my first visit. The building that currently houses YSPS is part of a long row of residential apartment buildings in downtown Yangon. I say "currently houses" because the school was forced to change locations each year of its existence. Once government authorities learned where the program had rented space they would refuse to grant the permits necessary to release the space the following year.

The street is narrow, residential, and crowded. Laundry flaps in the breeze for five floors. Men and women lean out on the small balconies to see who has arrived in the street or to talk to one another. Children play soccer barefooted in the street with their sandals set for the goal markers. Strings with clips hang down from the top floors, hovering above the ground, ready for deliveries. The YSPS doorway is unmarked and quite dark. I was convinced I was in the wrong place as I walked up the steep, dirty, and narrow staircase. Betel spit was in every corner. Finally, after arriving on the third floor, I came to a door marked Yangon

School of Political Science. Inside was a small lobby, two desks, and a few students. One went immediately to tell the director that I had arrived.

Political Prisoners Study Political Science

The YSPS Founder and Director, U Myat Thu, is a very kind, gentle man, and soft spoken political scientist. Myat Thu is, however, not an ordinary political science scholar. For nineteen years, he read politics, history, and theory in his prison cell. In 1988, Myat Thu was a young college student. The month Khin was born, he was arrested for demanding his right to speak freely. Myat Thu's father was one of the leaders of the 88 Uprising, but was fortunately not arrested. His younger brother was also arrested and served a long prison sentence. I asked Myat Thu about his mother's involvement in politics and he said, "my mother would tell us, 'you can smoke, you can drink, you can stay out all night, just don't do politics!'" For his involvement in 88 political protests, Myat Thu served the next nineteen years of his life in the Insein Prison and later in Bu Thee Taung prison, in a remote part of Rakhine state, for demanding his basic human rights. While in prison he taught himself English, and then he taught the language to other prisoners. Once in command of the language, he then directed his youngest brother (who followed his mother's wishes) to bring him political science and history books written in English. The guards could not read the English titles and only checked to make sure that the books had no markings of any kind. Myat Thus told me that the guards had been warned that political prisoner Nelson Mandela had used books and markings in those books to smuggle information of a sensitive nature to people outside the prison. Thus the guards only checked Myat Thu's books for possible communication with the outside world, not for the content of the books. Over time he amassed a substantial library.

In his prison cell, Myat Thu read John Locke, Alexis Tocqueville, Karl Marx, and many many other authors. He shared his books with his fellow political prisoners. He started teaching political science to a group of about ten prisoners with W. Phillips Shively's classic introductory reader in political science, "Power & Choice." Professor Shively's book is an easy to read, comparative, and conceptual introduction to political science. The book recounts dramatic and interesting stories of politics from all around the world. The theme of "power and choice" (how societies make decisions for different groups based on power or public choice), resonated with the political prisoners. The military government had certainly used power to deny the Burmese people their basic rights. Myat Thu and his prison mates studied politics as they lived in the wake of a violent and repressive government amid rats and horrible and unimaginable filth, with very little to eat, with the occasional snake falling from the ceiling onto their hard, uneven, and often muddy bamboo mats.

The prisoners' study of politics and history was richly ironic, as the Myanmar authorities had prohibited the study of political science outside the prison walls due to the perceived danger of the subject. The Myanmar generals so feared the study of political science that they even forbid students to study the discipline while abroad. The idea that the study of political science is dangerous is not limited to the Myanmar military. Nearly every legislative session, in recent years, a member of the Texas House of Representatives has introduced a bill that would eliminate the requirement for the study of political science in Texas colleges and universities. United States Senator Tom Coburn (R-Oklahoma) has worked hard since 2009 to restrict or eliminate the funding of political science research. Over those many years, Myat Thu and his fellow political prisoners read small libraries of political science and history books and they decided that if they were ever released that they would start a school to share what they had learned.

Myat Thu and his prison mates felt that a school was needed to provide a quality independent and uncensored political education to Myanmar students. In 2011, 2012, and 2013, as Myat Thu and his fellow self-trained political scholars were released from prison, the former political prisoners used what little money they could borrow from family to establish the Yangon School of Political Science. With his school established, Myat Thu formalized his own education with a graduate degree from the London School of Economics in 2013. In 2016, five years later, the thriving school now provides an outstanding graduate level political science program that is open to all interested students for a very small fee – about $20 USD per course. Today the school is largely funded by the United States National Endowment for Democracy and the United Kingdom's Department for International Development. In 2016, the school has taken on the mission of a political think-tank and a publishing house but has not yet been able to become accredited or even recognized by the Myanmar government as it is still viewed as dangerous and as a "political opposition establishment."

The day of my first class meeting, Htet Aung Lin, a YSPS staff member, met me outside my apartment and as we walked to get a taxi (YSPS took care of my travel to and from the school every day). He told me to call him Lin. Lin, a young man in his mid-twenties who regularly chews betel, told me that he is from Rakhine state and that his father is a poor fisherman. In that taxi ride (for more than hour) and during many others, Lin told me that his mother had kindled his interest in politics. In his formative years, his mother told him about the 88 Uprising and the deaths of many students who were fighting for democracy and human rights. His mother's stories glorified the student protestors. As an undergraduate student, Lin could not study political science, so he majored in History. During the 2007 Saffron Revolution, Lin joined in the protest at the Shwedagon Pagoda, was shot with rubber bullets, arrested, and imprisoned for six months. The incident only strengthened his resolve to study politics. Almost every student who attended my YSPS classes had a similar story.

Upon arrival at the school, Lin took me from the third floor YSPS offices up another steep and low (I had to duck) staircase to a small library. The library shelves looked like and were about the same size as those lining the shelves of a typical political science professor's office in the United States. The books were numbered and placed according to subject and region of the world. Many of the books were donated by Stanford University. When I left Myanmar, I also donated a few boxes of books. A doorway from the library led to the only classroom. The room is small, dark, but is always packed with enthusiastic political science students.

The YSPS students routinely attend lectures given by professors from all over the world. During the semester I taught at YSPS, the students also heard lectures from Drs. Larry Diamond and Francis Fukuyama from Stanford University. My YSPS class meetings were electric. The urgency of the topics – human rights, democracy, self-determination, racism, religion, and power filled the small makeshift classroom. Tears were not uncommon. Nodding heads and urgently shared stories about discrimination, repression, and even violence shaped and reshaped the hours we spent talking.

My YSPS students had lived political science and they intuitively understood the concepts that we American political science professors labeled and discussed in our lectures. These students had an excellent command of the US political system and were eager to apply it to Myanmar. They read every relevant book and constantly shared books with me on Facebook. Several YSPS students were planning to run for seats in the Myanmar Parliament (the Myanmar Constitution requires that twenty-five percent of the total members be from the Myanmar military).

Over time, we (the students and I) became a tribe, or band of brothers and sisters. Our discussions sometimes felt more like revolutionary meetings than the study of politics and policy. I will always be in touch with them, but Alison will tell you that the scene was tearful when it came time to say goodbye to my YSPS students.

Kissing the Earth with My Feet

Wearing my shoes, I came to a full stop at the doorway to the classroom of my very first teaching assignment in Myanmar. In the hall, outside the door, were some fifty pair of sandals lined up against the wall. Inside the classroom were some one-hundred bare feet. The British "shoe question" immediately came to mind. I was wearing my teaching shoes. I was also, in fact, wearing some wild socks. I wear comfortable shoes for support for the long hours of standing, walking, and lecturing on my feet. I add wild socks to the mix as one does want at least a hint of color. I, like the Brits, wear my shoes almost all the time. Back in Texas, I put them on first thing in the morning and wear them all day. I feel unprepared for work without them. Like the Brits, I feel somewhat exposed and vulnerable without my shoes. I hesitated at the door to my classroom, thinking about the British military officers who had refused to take off their boots when visiting the Shwedagon Pagoda.

Taking a deep breath, I thought, "I can do this, yes, I can and must be culturally sensitive. I can learn about and get to know this shoeless classroom, culture, and people." I took off my shoes and socks, and stepped into my first teaching experience in Myanmar, feeling somewhat bare and unprepared for the task at hand. Over the many months, teaching barefoot in Burma changed the way I thought about teaching, ethnocentricity, and about higher education. By the time I finished my year in Myanmar (and Thai) universities, I felt right at home teaching without my shoes.

One of my intentions in teaching is to be honest and genuine with my students. In order to be real, to be really honest, and to be trusted in the classroom (and elsewhere) one must *be* those things. Being open and authentic requires being vulnerable. Teaching barefoot accentuated my sense of vulnerability. Teaching barefooted in a very physical and direct way forced me to be grounded. Literally touching the floor allowed me to be mindful and present.

At his moment of enlightenment, the Buddha touched the earth with his right hand, and the stories tell that the Earth itself immediately responded: "I am your witness." Images of the Buddha often depict him sitting in meditation with his left hand, palm upright, in his lap, and his right hand touching the earth. The enlightenment of the Buddha, realized through his own efforts, was confirmed by his touching the earth. In a similar fashion, teaching with my feet touching "the earth" brought self-realization, honesty, and authenticity to the experience. It was awkward for a while, but in the end a gift.

The Buddha spent most of his adult life as a teacher. Alison bought me a beautiful "teaching Buddha" statute made from cedar wood. In teaching mode, the Buddha's right hand is turned palm out with thumb touching the first finger, while the left hand is touching the earth. The teaching Buddha statute is said to depict the Buddha's first lessons to monks after his enlightenment.

American-Centered Thinking

Teaching barefoot in Burma also revealed my American-centered thinking. Nearly all of the textbooks books I brought with me to Myanmar were written from an American point-of-view. Almost every PowerPoint slide that I had ever created was from that same world view. For more than two decades, I had been teaching about politics, religion, human rights and international relations from an American vantage point. In my comparative classes and in my international relations courses, I had always attempted to teach not only from an American perspective, but also from the point-of-view of the many other villages on this planet. But in preparing to teach my Myanmar courses, I became painfully aware of the dire need to reconsider and rework my lectures. Teaching in Myanmar forced me to rethink my approach to each course and even some concepts. I thought that since I would be teaching subjects that I had taught many times in the United States, it would not be time consuming, but I was incorrect. In order to make the material relevant and meaningful for my Myanmar students, I had to reorient every lecture. I had to find new examples and different readings. It was a laborious task. It was also thrilling, and a significant paradigm shift, and it turned out to be a focused learning experience to rethink and re-see the world from the Myanmar student's point-of-view. My Myanmar students also gave new life to ideas that my American students see as settled. For obvious reasons, my Myanmar students were acutely interested in democracy, human rights, and even fundamental concepts like sovereignty. Teaching in Myanmar gave me the gift of a new perspective, and it forced me to reconsider concepts that I had long thought I knew well and understood.

Cyclone Nargis

In the middle of the Yangon University campus is a huge and historic Thit Poke Pin tree. The seemingly dead, massive old tree, has long been regarded as a symbol of the Yangon University Students' resistance against the successive Myanmar military rulers. After tea at U Chit, students have gathered near the tree to protest. The legend and mystique of the tree grew when remarkably, the tree withstood the powerful Cyclone Nargis in 2008, when many other old trees in Yangon fell. On Friday, 2 May 2008, Cyclone Nargis caused the worst natural disaster in the recorded history of Myanmar. When the cyclone made landfall it sent a storm surge up the densely populated Irrawaddy delta, causing catastrophic destruction, and more than 138,000 fatalities. Millions of people were without power, basic healthcare, food, shelter, and drinking water for days. Many people died waiting for help. Sadly, international aid (from the United States and many other countries) for the cyclone victims was deliberately blocked by the military regime. The military did not want to appear to need outside or "foreign" help or support. For one of my students, Nargis was about more than a horrible natural disaster. It was a very personal example of an inexcusable state sovereignty.

One night in a YSPS class, I was leading a discussion about national sovereignty, which is routinely an "academic" argument in the United States. The issue for most American students and probably professors too, is an important but a largely settled matter of political life. Americans think that the people should be sovereign. A thirty-year-old student sitting on the front row asked, "when is it was acceptable for the United States or another country to ignore state sovereignty?" I paused before answering and he added, "In 2008 Myanmar was hit by a terrible cyclone, the worst disaster in our history. We could see US Navy ships offshore with supplies and water." Tears started to run down his cheeks, as he described the scene saying, "and our brothers and sisters (my little sisters) died while waiting for food and water. The government would not let the US Navy deliver the water and supplies." My Myanmar student, with tears streaming down his face, questioned a concept that most others think of as theoretical. Teaching barefoot in Burma was at times really hard...and all too real.

Re-Building Myanmar Higher Education

The US Embassy told me that I would be teaching at Yangon University several months before I arrived in Burma. I exchanged email with the Dr. Chaw Chaw Sein about my assignment and her teaching expectations. Oddly, I was unable to find out exactly when and what I would be teaching. Months went by and still I knew nothing. Finally, while teaching at YSPS, I scheduled a visit in the Yangon University International Relations Department. I did not meet with Dr. Chaw Chaw Sein, but instead met with a person, Anna Rogers [name changed], who had been hired by the Open Society Foundation to help recreate the curriculum in the political science department. Anna could not tell me exactly when classes would start nor when they would end. The military officials had not made that announcement. This was highly unusual for an American academic as we plan out our schedules two to five years in advance.

I knew that classes were to start sometime in late May or early June. Since I had not received any word on when I might be teaching, one morning in early June (on my way to buy groceries), I decided to walk over to campus to see if I could figure out when classes were to start. Completely unplanned, I walked into the International Relations office – where regularly ten women work (shuffling paper – really, actual paper – I have no idea what they do). They all stopped working and stood as I entered the office. Two women came over to me and asked what I needed (one went for coffee). I told them that I was wondering when my classes would be starting, what times, and days my classes would be meeting. They did not seem to understand my questions. So, I asked if they could show me the room where my classes would meet. They asked me to follow them. I followed them down a hallway, and they ushered me into a huge classroom full of students – my students! It was my class! It was about 10:35am and they had been sitting there waiting for me since 10:00am. As I had been uninformed of my schedule, of course, I had no idea. So, I put down my grocery sacks and started teaching, starting with the basics, we discussed "power." The students were very engaged and involved. A crowd gathered outside the room to listen – I invited them in – but they stayed in the hallway. After a while (I did not pay attention to the time) I asked them what time the class was over. They all said, "10:50." It was 11:58! There was not one peep or even a hint from them about being kept more than an hour past the end of class time. The crowd that had gathered in the hallway was the next class waiting on the crazy American to wrap up his lecture.

Seated to my right at a Thanksgiving table at the home of the United States Ambassador to Myanmar was a retired American university president. Seated to my left was the director of an international nongovernmental organization with a mission to help rebuild the entire education system in Myanmar. As is very often the case with academic administrators, the conversation turned to funding, faculty, buildings, and time. After his second glass of red wine, the president said, "To be really honest, guys, we cannot fix this system, rebuilding won't happen in my lifetime, it will take at least thirty to fifty years." The Myanmar education system – the entire system – is in ruins. Those with means send their children to private schools and then abroad for higher education. After fifty years of starving the education system of public funding, mistrusting academics, and intellectual pursuits, and literally destroying the system of education, the children and young adults people in Myanmar were left with little opportunity. The tendency of many academics who come to Myanmar (or other places around the world) is to attempt to champion change and "fix the system." One group of well-meaning academics from Johns Hopkins University attempted to do just that.

In 2013, Johns Hopkins University, initiated a series of well-funded programs at Yangon University that they designed to help Myanmar. Their efforts were extremely short-lived. Just one year later, in November 2014, Johns Hopkins abruptly cancelled the program, despite 67 students having been accepted into the program for 2015. When I arrived in Yangon in October of 2015, many Myanmar faculty wanted to complain and share stories about this failed project. Most people told me that Johns Hopkins did not work closely and respectfully with the Myanmar Ministry of Education nor did the Ministry of education agree to the Johns Hopkins administrators' demand for total academic freedom. In order to facilitate change, an assessment must be undertaken to determine the actual needs, rather than projecting and implementing preconceived plan of what some may deem as best practice. Johns Hopkins failed to include Myanmar officials and administrators in the creation and development of programs, expecting the Ministry of Education and Yangon University to agree to whatever they proposed. According to the Myanmar Times, one person who was part of the project said, "Just because you are giving someone something, you can't assume they are going to grab it like a candy bar. There was a lack of inter-institutional buy-in and coordination between the two universities and there were different expectations about what was needed. An in-depth discussion about how the center fit into the university's goals and aims, and that never took place. As a Fulbrigher, it's best to share when asked, and to do a great deal of listening and learning before answering.

Well-meaning academic leaders, like Myat Thu, and Dr. Chaw Chaw Sein, are leading the way and have begun the process of rebuilding and creating a system of education, but it is still in the very early stages. Dr. Chaw Chaw Sein asked me to read and edit a lengthy and well considered report she wrote for the Ministry of Education. In her report, she has outlined outstanding and exciting plans. The next steps will be to find support to rebuild the foundations for great institutions. I hope that future Fulbright scholars will invest time and energy supporting those plans for the higher education programs across the country, and the wonderful Myanmar students. The work was hard. Another Fulbright scholar said, "teaching in Myanmar is like a Peace Corps assignment." I suffered and yes, I worked extremely hard, but I was extremely fortunate to learn from and with my Myanmar tribe. Teaching barefoot in Burma, being immersed in an entirely foreign classroom, allowed me to clearly see my discipline and myself.

Homage Ceremony

The morning of my last day in the Yangon University classroom, I put on a traditional Myanmar collared shirt and a beautiful longyi my teaching assistants had given me the day before. A longyi is surprisingly comfortable. I took the students a gift of candy (they had requested "gummi bears") and we reviewed for their final exam. After the review, the students told me that they wanted to perform a traditional Buddhist "Homage Ceremony." In ancient Myanmar culture, teachers are one component of the "five revered ones," along with the Buddha, dhamma (teachings of the Buddha), the sangha (the order of monks) and parents. I was told a few days before that my students would "pay respect" to me, but I had no idea what that would mean. I learned later that the homage ceremony is traditionally performed only once a year (in October), but my students wanted to do it for me before I left Myanmar. At first, I did not understand the seriousness of their expression of respect. It was a solemn ceremony. Barefooted and wearing a longyi, following my student's direction, I stood on stage, while they all got on their knees in the aisles between the desks. In unison, they raised their prayer hands to their foreheads, bowed three times, while chanting an ancient message of gratitude and reverence. In Burmese, they said, "We raise our joined hands in reverence to the forehead and worship, honor, look at, and humbly pay homage to you our teacher, once, twice, and three times." After they finished, I expressed my heartfelt gratitude for the privilege of learning with them. The ceremony ended with the presentation of a number of beautiful gifts. I have never been so honored by a group of students.

Yangon University Honors students pay respect to Robert Sterken (2016).
Photo credit: Robert Sterken.

Chapter 7

Burma Lessons: The Noble Eightfold Path

◊

The Impermanence of Autumn Rain

The rains fell, just as I was told they would. It rained almost continuously for three months. The Myanmar rainy season brought monsoon rains like I had never experienced. The rain danced off the tin awning over the balcony where Hjar Hjar and I visited. Huge drops woke me in the middle of the night and fell on me as I walked to class. Myanmar is lovely in the rainy season, it's cooler, green, and beautiful. An umbrella is needed every day. The rains came down just as Forrest Gump described, "One day it started raining, and it didn't quit for four months. We been through every kind of rain there is. Little bitty stingin' rain, and big ol' fat rain. Rain that flew in sideways. And sometimes rain even seemed to come straight up from underneath. Shoot, it even rained at night."

I love the Burma rains. Rain has always been a signal – to me anyway – of reprieve. Rain quiets my mind and gray skies seem to wrap all in a healing respite. When it rains, I can take a breath. Rain brings relief from the heat of activity. No hay can be hauled, no real work can be done on a farm, while it rains. Life, of course, depends on rain. From the mud, life awakens. We need its renewing. The Burma rains in June, July, and August of 2016 renewed my spirit. As they have for eternity, the Burma rains made the tropical greens deep, the frogs loud, and the noises of the jungle vibrate with life. Sitting on my balcony with Hjar Hjar, I recorded those sounds one night and sent them to my sons and daughter. The Burma rainy season brought peace and renewed hope to the sun drenched land, it flooded the rice fields, and it brought change. The Pali Cannon states that like the impermanence of autumn rain, everything changes. Life was changing in Myanmar, democracy was in the air, and I would be going home at the end of the rainy season, changed by a year among the generous and beautiful people of Myanmar.

The Rainy Season

During the Buddha's later life, a group of monks from Burma set out to see him and to sit at his feet for instruction. Unfortunately, the monks embarked upon the journey during the rainy season – the time of flooding the rice fields – and none of the roads were paved. The monks walked in the monsoon rains and winds, and through rice fields for many days. Upon their arrival they were in no condition to learn from the Buddha as they were exhausted, hungry, wet, and covered in mud. Rice farmers along the monk's route were unhappy that the monks had trampled their rice. As a result, the Buddha declared that monks and nuns must not make any journey, lasting longer than one night, during the rainy season. To this day, Buddhist monks do not very often travel during the rainy season (I did see a few in airports).

The rainy season is the Buddhist Lent. Like the Christian Lent, the Buddhist Lent is a time of prayer or meditation, self-examination, devotion, and reflection. Also, like Christians, Buddhists volunteer their time and give of themselves to others more deeply during Lent. The rainy season in Myanmar lasts for three months, those months are especially holy, and the Myanmar people devote the time to doing good deeds for others and their community. Monks deliver many day-long sermons in community centers. Sermons can often be heard in taxis. Like a Southern Baptist tent revival, Monks set up stages with flowers and loud speakers and deliver sermons for hours (sometimes for eight or ten hours at a time) for the entire community. Many Myanmar Buddhists eat strictly a vegetarian diet during these three months. The pagodas and monasteries are also more crowded during the rainy months. It was during the rainy season that I wrote most of this book. My time in Myanmar taught me so much about the people and cultures of the country, but it also reshaped the way I think about Americans. This is hard to explain, but it is one of the more important lessons of my Fulbright.

Cultural Sensitivity

I came to view the people in the United States differently. As a person who regularly travels, I well understand the importance of being culturally sensitive. To be culturally sensitive means to be aware of cultural differences without assigning them a value, either positive or negative, better or worse, right or wrong. As I came to know my Myanmar students and friends, I began to appreciate not only our cultural differences, but also the many similarities with Americans back home. For example, the poor people in Myanmar are very similar to poor people in East Texas. Both lack education, are often very religious, and struggle with the day-to-day basics needed to survive. They all want the best for their children, and many have high hopes for tomorrow. As I visited the villages and met the Myanmar poor, the "grassroots" people, I felt a sense of connection, our common humanity, and came to see the people in my own village back in the United States in a new light. I felt a deepened sense of respect for my own people. I came to be more culturally sensitive in reverse. For example, I came to think about some of my American students a little differently.

At my home university on occasion a well-meaning and or suspicious student will stop by during office hours and ask if I am a Christian, or more often, if I "have accepted Jesus into my heart." They are usually concerned about my soul, but sometimes just do not want to be taught by a person who does not share their beliefs. Over the years, my approach to that question has been to respond gently and sensitively to the young person's question, but to not give a specific answer.

Interestingly, I received the very same question in Myanmar, but with much greater frequency. Most Myanmar students and people I met, assumed I was a Christian and wanted confirmation. My first teaching assignment in Myanmar was in a private Christian (Baptist) college and the students on that campus were not at all shy about asking about my faith. I followed my pattern of responding, without really answering. While at Yangon School of Political Science several students assumed I was Muslim, as I passionately and fiercely defended the rights of the Myanmar Muslim minority.

Finally, when I moved to Yangon University the question came up yet again, only this time it was being asked by Theravada Buddhists (there were only two Muslim students in my YU classes). The Buddhist students also assumed that I was a Christian. For a reason I cannot exactly identify, my Myanmar students made me think about not only the tribal labels we cling to so tightly, but also the frail and vulnerable individual living in the United States who is also living within the confines of his or her life experiences. Poignantly, this insight made me more understanding and respectful of our shared human hopes and fears.

The people of Myanmar and the United States, perhaps I should just say people of the world, share many of the same hopes and troubles. Both societies are suffering with gross inequality, structural racism, and fear. Many humans fear "others," and also many cling to and act upon their ignorance and the resulting fear of vulnerability and insecurity. Many people in Myanmar and in the United States fear the unknown and the loss of their way of life. They fear the loss of their religion. Globalization and the spread of ideas is reshaping our global village. I heard this fear expressed during interviews with monks, conversations with taxi drivers, and long visits with locals in tea shops in Myanmar. I regularly heard it in the conversations with my working-class students from Dallas and Longview, Texas. Whether eating at a Dairy Queen in deep East Texas or a tea shop in Mandalay, the workers discuss lazy people (lots of Myanmar people told me that "the Burmese are lazy"), the rich just keep getting richer, and working people are on the losing end of the global economic and political systems. The people of Myanmar recently elected a new government and, although real hope is in the air, there are still many who are fearful and cling to the ideas of "protecting race and religion." Despite their self-labeled racial differences, people in villages on opposite sides of the planet share the very same sense of uncertainty. We all face suffering, challenges, and wicked problems. The teachings of the Buddha provide the Myanmar people with a wise and compelling guide, the Eightfold Path, to addressing challenges and problems.

The Eightfold Path

The Buddha's teachings were in part, about living with problems, uncertainties and suffering. In fact, the Buddha suggested an Eightfold Path for, not necessarily overcoming, but alleviating suffering. There is a great deal of wisdom in the Buddha's Eightfold Path, as it is centered upon time honored principles. The eight components of this path are not in any specific order, instead they are interrelated and interdependent components. Each step includes the practice of the others. My time in Myanmar provided some insight into this Eightfold Path. The Path has been written about in many other places, but I came to see it as following eight habits of mind and heart and it illustrates some important insights I learned during my year in Myanmar. The Path includes, 1) Right Understanding, 2) Right Intent, 3) Right

Speech, 4) Right Action, 5) Right Livelihood, 6) Right Effort, 7) Right Mindfulness, and 8) Right Concentration.

1. Right View

The Eightfold Path suggests that we must see the world as it actually is (not as we are or as we want it to be). This is not a simple task, but it was made easier for me by living in a foreign land. I do not think that foreign travel is necessary to achieve this habit, but I do think that it makes understanding and seeing from a different point-of-view a great deal easier. In Myanmar, I "saw" my American-centered lectures in a new light and I came to see race differently. Pretending to not see (taking the wrong view) the construction and artificial nature of race does not mean that it does not exist. Pretending that we do not see the problems and injustices of the race issue or any other issue is willful ignorance. The first practice of the Eightfold Path is to observe the world around us as it actually is, not as we want it to be. The "right view" is to practice being intellectually honest with ourselves and with others. We must be willing to give up what we know in order to gain a new perspective.

2. Right Intentions

The second habit of Eightfold Path is that of being mindful and aware of our intentions towards ourselves and others. Being mindful and aware of my own intentions allowed me to be more at ease with not knowing and not understanding the cultural norms and practices in Myanmar. I knew that I intended respect, even if I accidentally blundered backwardly into disrespect. Myanmar Buddhists recite the daily prayer of metta. With this prayer, they wish and the intention is that all sentient beings be well. What a spectacular intention. The version I recited, (May all live in happiness. May all be safe. May all be healthy in mind and body. May all beings live in peace and harmony), set my intention. According to the Eightfold Path, the right intention leads to right action.

3. Right Action

The third practice of the Eightfold Path is to pay attention to our actions, to make sure that our actions are for good, and that they do not harm ourselves or others. Again, the mindful practice of giving, sets in motion a ripple of actions that changes the nature of the Myanmar society. The right action brings about goodwill all across the country. The Buddha's instructions on "the right action" were to work for the happiness of others. The Buddha said, "Go your way, oh monks, for the benefit of many, for the happiness of many, out of compassion for the world, for the good, benefit and happiness of gods and men." The Buddhists are a kind people and make a regular practice of giving. There is amazing power in a kind word, a touch, or a just a smile. This third practice of the Eightfold Path instructs us to take account of our actions, that we must – in our every action – act for good and against what we know to be wrong. With right views, right intentions, and right actions, we can fight against poverty, brutality, give comfort, and even challenge evil.

Right action can also be inaction; it can be doing less or nothing at all. I had to learn to slow down in Myanmar. Well, at least I learned to dance within the cadence of Myanmar life. I was not able to do all of the things I thought I needed to do. By striving to do too much, my actions (or attempted actions) were harming my health and sense of well-being. I also learned that inaction can be good. Every day in Myanmar, I saw people engaged in inaction. They were doing nothing. I was surprised nearly every day to see men from my apartment building just sitting with one another for long periods of time. Americans are typically taught to shun in-action; we are taught to gauge our value by our productivity, but in doing so we are denied the simple sweetness and re-creation of doing nothing.

4. Right Words

The fourth practice of the Eightfold Path is the habit of communicating without harming (intentionally making people angry), with honesty, and without deceptive language. Dishonesty harms others and ourselves. The hateful language of the Myanmar monk, Wirathu, who preaches of the need to "protect race and religion" is harming many others. Words matter. A thoughtful and kind word can mean so very much. The Myanmar shop owner who called me his brother warmed my lonely heart. Simple words can send waves of love or sow the seeds of discord and suffering. The faculty member who told me that it was okay to feel awkward and clumsy in my new culture gave me the great gift of ease. Using the right words (kind communication) does not mean that we do not express opposing opinions or that we must not engage in conflict, rather it is the practice of considering whether our words will do harm – more harm than good. Will that Facebook rant harm or hurt? Is the intention positive or too critical, kind, or mean-spirited?

5. Right Occupation

The fifth practice of alleviation of suffering relates to the way a person spends his or her time. This component suggests that we occupy our time with endeavors that do not harm others. Our work should not harm others. While there is much to discuss around this practice, my notions of what it means to have the right livelihood changed somewhat in Myanmar. Just as in the United States, I saw people engaged in occupations that many Americans would not classify as "successful."

Nearly every day on my way to my campus, I passed a vendor, a rotund Myanmar woman whose cart was located on the corner not far from my apartment. Her occupation, selling boiled corn-on-the-cob, would without a doubt be viewed as unsuccessful by many Americans. But her work, while not complicated, was helpful to her village, and certainly not harmful. She was happily engaged with her community. Nearly every day, as I passed her corner, I saw her laughing and visiting with someone as she served them a hot ear of corn. I took her photograph several times over the year and she came to laugh and wave when she saw me. In the following photo she turned, smiled, and waved on her way to her post on corner.

Corn-on-the-cob vendor (2016). Photo credit: Robert Sterken.

Myanmar pushed me to rethink occupation and success. The typical societal version of success is defined along a pretty narrow spectrum and that spectrum does not always include the "right occupation" for each of us. According to the Buddha's Eightfold Path, our success and right occupation is what is good and best for us and non-harming to others. We must follow our own passions (not those of others) in a way that respects and nurtures our true self. Following one's passions is a not a simple task in the United States, and much less so in Myanmar. Nearly sixty years of repressive military rule and closed schools have left many people uneducated and with few real options. But as with Myat Thu and his study of political science shows, it is really very hard to suppress a determined person – even one in a muddy prison cell. Once a person finds his right occupation everything seems to work out, even in the most difficult of places on earth.

However, the reality also dictates that many of my Myanmar students and those in the generations before, like Khin, simply did not have the opportunity to follow whatever dreams they wanted. One of my Yangon University students, nicknamed Nick, wanted to be a fashion photographer. His parents and older siblings were all working to support him at Yangon University. His father wanted him to go into government service, thus his enrollment in my political science course, where he would have a small ($200 a month) salary and a secure life. Parents want security for their children. Nick is a very bright, outgoing person, and has a wonderful command of the English language. His Facebook page shows him to be a talented photographer and he dreams of going to San Francisco or New York to study photography, but, his real world situation has placed significant barriers in his way. While his dreams are not impossible, it is important to note that we do not all share the same set of opportunities – even within the United States. There is a tendency to think that really all that is needed to accomplish dreams and goals is grit and determination – and like Myat Thu – one can assume his or her right occupation. Many people believe that everyone deserves or has earned their achieved station and occupation. That is simply not true. We have a belief in fairness, justice, and equality combined with deep and systemic inequality. It is just wrong of us to judge a person's value by his or her

"success" or occupation. Our village needs the lady
selling corn-on-the-cob on the corner of Insein Road.
Our souls need a kinder – less-judgmental – non-
harming view of occupation, just as our bodies need
the food that is sold on the corner.

6. Right Effort

Ralph Waldo Emerson described "right effort" when
he wrote, "Sow a thought and you reap an action; sow
an act and you reap a habit; sow a habit and you reap
a character; sow a character and you reap a destiny."
In Myanmar I put my efforts into writing, teaching
and research. I also leaned into or accepted the
discomfort; I learned the futility of fighting against
that which I could not change. I directed my efforts
and focus on learning and on finding my way in a
very foreign land. I deliberately took off my shoes,
wiped the sweat from my glasses, struggled with the
language, and taught my classes. The essence of the
sixth principle in the Eightfold Path is that we reap
what we sow. If one wants to harvest rice he must
prepare the soil, plant the seed, flood and nurture the
growing rice plants. All of these steps absolutely must
be taken before rice can grow and ultimately be
harvested. The law of the harvest is simple; the work
must be done.

The principle of the harvest – one reaps what one
sows – is part of the writings of all major religions
and is found in every culture. The Bible, in Galatians,
states that "whatever one sows, that will he also
reap." For Buddhists, reaping what one sows is about
the consequences of one's actions. The Myanmar
people believe that if one is kind they will reap what

they have sown. All major religions teach kindness and charity, but the people of Myanmar, like many Americans, act to practice that value.

One day, I took a photo of a young nun who was out gathering alms, she was perhaps ten or twelve years old. I used the photo in a slide in a class discussion about global inequality with my students at Yangon University. To facilitate the discussion, I broke the students into groups of three and asked them to discuss the possible life story of the girl in the photo. How had she become a nun? After some time, I took up their written reports of their group discussion and we had a full class conversation about the young nun. My student's thoughts surprised me. They explained that she (like almost all nuns and novices) was most likely from a very poor family, a family too poor to care for her, and so she lived in a monastery. I expected that conclusion, but it was the next thing they all collectively agreed upon and said that astonished me. They said, "it is our culture to take care of the poor." The students explained that they felt not only a sense of duty, but that society took daily action to meet the needs of the five hundred thousand members of the monastic community. Actions matter.

Right efforts matter. In the book of Hosea in the Bible we are told that if, "you have plowed wickedness, you reap injustice." The intolerant Myanmar monks who have focused their actions and communications on intolerance and hate have indeed sown seeds of division and violence. Americans leaders who sow the seeds of hate and intolerance do the very same. In the Bible, Job 4:8 says, "As I have observed, those

who plow evil and those who sow trouble reap it."
From those seeds grow fear, mistrust, and insecurity.
Again, U Wirathu, who preaches of the need to
"protect race and religion" is sowing fear and hate in
his community. Wirathu's own suffering is spilling
over into his village in the form of fear and violence.

The sixth practice of the Eightfold Path tells us to
focus on right efforts. That means we must let go of
our fears and insecurity. We must accept, learn, and
face the things we are scared to face. We have the
option to write a wonderful story, or a story of fear,
insecurity and hiding. We all have the option to
choose right action, even if like, Ko Ko Gyi, we were
born in country with a ruthless military government
and little opportunity.

7. Right Mindfulness

The Buddha's seventh practice for alleviating our
suffering is right mindfulness. The Buddha taught a
simple truth, life is only available in the present
moment. Living in the past only leads to suffering
with our unchangeable history. The past is gone and
cannot be changed no matter how much we
perseverate and suffer over it. On the other hand, the
future is not yet here. Worrying about or suffering
over the future is nearly as futile as regretting the
past. As Jesus told his followers, "Never worry about
tomorrow, because tomorrow will worry about itself.
Each day has enough trouble of its own." If we live in
the past or in the future, we cannot really be fully
present and in touch with real life. Right mindfulness
is the practice of being focused on this moment and
aware of the beauty in this specific moment. To live

in the present, does not mean that we do not ever think about the past or plan for our futures. We should learn from our past. Our history is important and much insight can be derived by looking into our past. But we are far more than the sum of our history and regrets and while we can appreciate and even mourn the past, life can only be lived in the present. We must also plan for our futures. The seventh practice of mindfulness is the realization that being lost in regret about the past is futile and that worrying about our futures is pointless suffering.

Some people say that when taking photos people are not enjoying the present moment. I disagree. I think that the focus of the eyes on the present scene, event, or person is indeed being mindful of the moment. Mindfully take photos of all you see, but be there while doing it. Alison's photo of the monk smoking a cigar while playing chess was a focus on that very beautiful moment. Taking photos of my students while they worked encapsulated my focus on that beautiful moment.

My bare feet on the classroom floors in Myanmar also brought me the moment, leading me to focus mindfully on the present. In many religions, bare feet are seen as a sign of humility and it is common to remove shoes when entering a holy place. When entering a Buddhist pagoda, a mosque or a Hindu temple, visitors remove their shoes to be respectful, humble, and present. In my Myanmar classrooms my bare feet were a message of humility, respect, and sameness. Being mindful in my teaching was a subtle shift in my approach. Being mindfully grounded in the present moment in my classrooms, allowed for a deepened awareness and concentration.

8. Right Concentration

At the top of the notes I take to class with me, I regularly write, "smile, breathe and go slowly." I set the intention to concentrate on the students, lesson, and the classroom experience. The eighth practice of the Eightfold Path is focus. Too often we allow our minds to address a multitude of different tasks or ideas at once. Right concentration is the polar opposite of the Western notion of multitasking. Scholars have shown in many recent studies that quality of work declines when students attempt to multitask, because the brain can truly focus on only one task at a time. Laptops and other digital devices in the classroom erode the learning experience. My Myanmar students did not have internet access (it is just not available) while in the classrooms, most could not afford laptops, and thus the experience was significantly different from my American classrooms. As a result of teaching in Myanmar, I may change my policy about student's access to digital devices in my classrooms. My American students now must take notes, by hand, just like my Myanmar students (I will still allow them to wear their shoes).

Right concentration is learned through mindfulness meditation. Meditation teaches us how to be calm and to focus on one specific thing or on nothing at all. Learning is made possible with a calm and focused mind. If one's mind is wandering, she is simply not present for the lesson. At the beginning of most of my classes, I regularly turn the lights off, and ask my students to, "be here now," and then to take a few slow and deep calming breaths (I model this for them). I want them to relax into the room and space in order to be ready to learn. My American students sometimes laugh at this, but my Myanmar students, especially the Yangon University Buddhist students, well understand my intention and the practice. The nature of the classroom changed and the students were more present. The seventh and eighth practices of concentration and mindfulness sharpen the mind, brings it to the present.

Promotion of Good Will

While the Eightfold Path itself requires concentration, mindfulness, and a lifelong practice, the rewards are substantial. The Path does not put an end to all suffering, but when practiced it does bare the fruit of a more peaceful, calm, and happy life. Perhaps this is why so many people have noted the "happy-go-lucky" nature of the people of Myanmar. In spite of being among the world's poorest people, they are not only happy but also the most generous. They enjoy the fruits of the principles of the Eightfold Path. The very intention of the Fulbright Program is in keeping with the Buddha's principles and teachings. In September 1945, the freshman senator from Arkansas, J. William Fulbright, wrote and introduced a bill in the United States Congress.

In keeping with the Eightfold Path, Fulbright's bill created a program that sought "promotion of international good will." It is a little thing, but as I walked down the streets in Yangon, I smiled, I stopped to add a bit of money to a beggar's bowl, I responded to the many sing-song English hellos with

my own singing hello, or with Mingalaba, and in a
small way helped to promote Senator Fulbright's
intention of good will. As people from buses "looked
deeply" at the tall white skinned foreigner, I smiled. I
cheerfully agreed to pose for selfies taken with many
strangers.   In thousands of small ways Senator
Fulbright's plan of cross-cultural exchange worked
well every day in Myanmar. Every year many
Fulbright scholars travel throughout the world
sending ripples of good will with teaching, research,
and with smiles. According to the United States State
Department, the Fulbright Program sends about 8,000
Fulbrighters abroad each year. Roughly 1,600 U.S.
students go abroad, 4,000 foreign students come to
the United States, and about 1,200 U.S. professors
travel to share and learn with the citizens of the
countries to which they are assigned. Since Senator
Fulbright acted to promote good will in 1945, about
310,000 "Fulbrighters" have participated in the
Program in almost all of the countries of the world.
Goodwill does not always come in the form we
expect. At the end of a long day a tuk tuk driver (a tuk
tuk is a rickshaw, in this case a motorcycle pulling a
cart) in Bangkok said, "If you are happy, I am
happy."

Taken for a Ride

While in Bangkok before my lecture to the Thai
Princess, I went shopping for a jacket. I wanted a
traditional straight cut jacket with what some call a
Nehru collar or a Chinese collar. The jacket is popular
all across Asia. I went to an unbelievably large
shopping mall, appropriately named the "World
Market Center," which houses seven floors of

shopping and dining. I shopped for this special jacket for a few hours, but could only find very expensive versions – jackets in the $1000 USD range. Tired and giving up, I walked out of the mall to find a taxi. Waiting at the exit was a Thai man in a tuk tuk who asked me if I wanted a ride. I said, "no, just waiting for a taxi." I was tired and did not feel like a ride in a trailer pulled by a motorcycle. While I waited for a taxi and he ask me where I was going. Being polite but not giving much information, I just said, "back to my hotel." Not relenting, he said, "I will take you for half the taxi fare and quicker." He explained that he could go a route that cars could not. Bangkok traffic is legendarily slow, so I reluctantly agreed and off we went.

When we came to a stop at the first traffic light, he said, "I need to stop by my boss's office, it's just on the way, and won't take but a second." Again, just being polite, I agreed. It was starting to be an interesting ride. With a breeze in my face, we went down one-way streets the wrong way and through back alleys. At one point, a guard raised a traffic arm and waved us through a hotel back alley and the driver then cut in front of a full line of traffic by circling from a one-way street in a crosswalk. Finally, he stopped in front of a steep set of stairs which I could not see because the top of the tuk tuk was so low. My driver said, "I won't be but a few minutes, I need to get a gas coupon from my boss. Look around in this shop and I will be waiting when you are ready." The shop he suggested I look into was a tailor shop. I climbed out of the tuk tuk and I was greeted at the door of the tailor shop by "Michael" (a name to suit Westerners no doubt) a diminutive man in a brown three-piece suit and a measuring tape draped around his neck. I later learned that Michael is from Karen state in Myanmar. Michael asked, "How can I help sir?" I told him that coincidentally, my driver had stopped in front of his shop and I that I just wanted to look around. Michael said, "the driver works for me, I give him gas and he brings me customers." I was immediately worried about a scam and also about the "foreigner's price." Michael's shop was large, clean, and full of beautiful materials – large bolts of cloth. He made clothes for women and men. I told him that oddly, in fact, I was looking for a specific jacket and described it to him. Of course, Michael knew just the jacket. He walked me over to a huge rack of material and asked me what color I had in mind. I pointed out a navy material, but explained that I would be leaving Bangkok in two days. "No problem, I can have this jacket made and delivered to your hotel tomorrow evening at 8pm." We looked at several different fabrics- ranging in price. With a fabric I liked, the jacket would cost just $80 USD. I agreed thinking, "even if I never see a jacket, or if it's horrible and just a rag, I've learned a lesson and got a fun little story to tell."

While taking my measurements, Michael and I talked about Myanmar and his clients from the US Embassy in Yangon. With no hint of considering their privacy, he brought out his order book and showed me the names of men from the US Embassy in Yangon who had recently placed orders with him. After he finished taking my measurements he asked me to come upstairs with him. He wanted to show me more expensive materials. He wanted me to upgrade the material in my jacket. I laughed, and said no that this was enough of an adventure already.

My tuk tuk driver, who said his name was Jack, was still waiting for me. He wanted to know how much I had ordered as he received more gas for bigger orders. On the way back to the hotel he wrote his name and number down for me and said that the ride was free. I laughed saying "not really," as I had just bought a jacket from his boss. The next evening after my day-long event with the Thai Princess, I wondered if the jacket would actually turn up and what it might look like. At 8:45pm, forty-five minutes late, the hotel bellhop delivered my beautiful new jacket with the Nehru collar. Yes, I probably paid the "foreigner's price." I was manipulated and one could say that I was "taken." Being new to a culture or system is okay, not knowing is okay. I rolled with the adventure, the wild ride, and Jack, my tuk tuk driver, and I shared Senator Fulbright's good-will and a laugh.

Yangon's Circle Train

The Fulbright allowed me to visit with many people and see many places in Burma and all across Southeast Asia. I spent time with monks in Mandalay, drank beer with former political prisoners, talked politics with young activists, had tea with students and coffee with faculty, and talked with old men in streets. I met what many people would consider "important people." One day, in the last weeks of my year in Burma, three of my YSPS students asked me to take a ride with them on the Yangon circle train. I had ridden the train with Alison and my daughter and was not really interested in riding it again, but they were determined to show me the people of Myanmar and so off I went.

During that four-hour bone-rattling train ride, I met a Canadian couple who were both in their early seventies. They were very friendly, open, and as we were sitting quite close together we began to visit. While watching the scenes of the lives of the people both on the train and in the countryside go by, we shared sketches of our life stories. They were both professionals, she was a lawyer and he was a retired executive from a large multinational firm. It was odd, in a way, chatting with people from a world of wealth and privilege while riding the Yangon circle train. For a few hours they told me about their careers and lives. She reminded me of the Buddha's teachings when she said, "young man, a lifetime goes by like a flash of lightning."

While we talked, we rocked through Myanmar daily life, dinner tables, tea shops, places of burial, folk religion alters placed high in trees, mothers carrying newborn babies, children playing soccer, and a great deal of suffering. The rattling and rocking of the train, the scenes of the poorest people, passengers moving about and getting on and off, the heat, smoke from coal fires, and the out-of-place conversation with the Canadian couple, made it all feel dreamlike. It was as if I was watching the movements of a wild dance, the dance of life. The couple had retired and taken up travel. They explained that were "cycling all of Asia." They looked fit and healthy, but I was really impressed by their undertaking, and I knew a thing or two about the dangers of cycling in Myanmar. At her urging the husband took his iPad from his backpack and began to show me photos of the two of them with their bikes in different places around the world. They traveled with and rode very expensive bikes with lots of gear. He said, "we wanted to see new people, experience new places and eat new foods. There is a whole different world waiting out there to be discovered, and we just want to see it before we can't." The next morning, they were to join up with a group and a guide for the long ride from Yangon to Bagan. After they arrived in the ancient Buddhist kingdom, they would be taking a balloon over the Bagan pagodas and drinking wine in the ancient Buddhist lands. The wife said, "yes, sometimes cycling that far is really hard, I have crashed my bike more than once and ended up in the hospital a couple of times, but we do not want to live as though we are already dead." I gave them my card, they promised to email (they never did). I expect that they are now cycling somewhere near Angor Wat or about to set out to cycle from Pamplona on the famous route of St. James.

The Movements of the Dance

I started writing this book to answer the seemingly simple question about how my year in Burma changed me. How does one make sense of it all? I am not sure I know of the many ways the fabric of my soul has changed. I do know that I will enjoy the sights, the people who I came to know as friends, the many awkward experiences, the meals I ate, and even the difficulties for the rest of my life. I believe that we absolutely must join in and accept the pure pleasure of this surreal dance. I willingly put myself squarely in the middle of melting heat, endless rain, creature discomforts, many embarrassing situations, culture shock, and struggle to experience the dance. I was willing to struggle and suffer to see and experience a world beyond my own. Like my Canadian friends, I did not want to live life like the walking dead.

I learned from the beautiful people of Myanmar that we cannot and should not wait until we are no longer suffering before we allow ourselves to live and to be happy. The people of Burma are all too well acquainted with suffering, as they have lived in poverty under fifty-five years of an oppressive military regime. They taught me about suffering, and like the Buddha, taught me how to alleviate or at least to tolerate suffering. While there is obviously much wisdom in their experiences and in the Buddha's Eightfold Path, there is also real beauty and much to be gained in the struggle. During my time abroad my son compared my journey to Homer's Odysseus (although, unlike Telemachus, my son did not have to deal with a group of unruly suitors). Like Odysseus, I am "a man who has been through bitter experiences and travelled far and even come to enjoy his sufferings after a time."

I left the creature comforts of Tyler, Texas and made a life on the other side of the earth. While teaching barefoot in Burma, I gave my heart to my students and to the people. They will forever be part of me. Living abroad changed my notion of what it means to be "home" and of "nationalism." Borders, citizenship, and passports mean little when you a have real connections in a far off lands. Maybe this is what Senator Fulbright hoped would happen.

In my last days in Myanmar, I said my goodbyes, gave away all my books, promised to be back soon, and Hjar Hjar and I talked over one final painful Buddhist lesson. I hate goodbyes and Hjar Hjar was struggling with attachment, he did not want to see me go. Late on my last night in Yangon, we sat on the balcony watching it rain, sharing a parting beer. I sat in the curved teak wood chair the MIT students gave me and Hjar Hjar listened from one of my potted plants. We talked about the Buddhist principle of change. I told him that our every encounter, the sharing of the dance of our lives, is brief and must be treasured. I reminded him that the Buddha said, "this existence of ours is as transient as autumn rains. To watch the birth and death of beings is like looking at the movements of a dance. A lifetime is like a flash of lightning in the sky, rushing by, like a torrent down a steep mountain." The next day I boarded a flight home to Texas and left Hjar Hjar in the embrace of the generous and kind care of the beautiful people of Myanmar.

Robert Sterken on the Yangon train (2016). Photo credit Than Toe Aung.

Epilogue

◊

Everything Changes

One of the fundamental teachings of Buddhism is the impermanence of everything. Everything changes. The things I saw and experienced in Southeast Asia in 2015-2016 will be different today and different yet again tomorrow. It is my hope that my humble insights and the lessons I learned will help others. The history I have recorded in these pages should help others understand what it was like and how living and teaching barefoot in Burma changed me. But it is important to note that even history changes. I have only recorded the dance as I saw it in 2015-2016. You will see a different dance. Go be part of it!

There are many self-congratulating travel writers and tourists from all over the world who write about Myanmar today. Many write that they came to Myanmar "just-in-time" to see the country before the Chinese, Japanese, and Americans paved the it over with California-like malls and Western lifestyle and comforts. If one flies into Yangon, takes a taxi to an expensive hotel, sees only the Shwedagon Pagoda, Bogyoke Market, jets up to Bagan for hot air balloon ride over the pagodas, and then finally spends a day or two in Mandalay, he will indeed see some beautiful and wonderful sights. Afterward, he could, as many do, easily write that he saw the "real Burma" just before it changed. He would, of course, be correct. However, he would only be correct because everyone who sees anything, sees it right before it changes. Cultures evolve, people change, religions change, cities change, countries change – everything changes.

Yes, Myanmar is also changing, and today travelers can travel to Yangon and stay in a beautiful and comfortable hotel. One can travel to Mandalay and never really see the local people or their coal cooking fires and bamboo sleeping mats. A person with means can live in modern air-conditioned Myanmar. While seated in comfortable leather seats of an SUV, she can look through the smoked glass, only catch glimpses of the lives many lead. I have witnessed this. In my year in Myanmar, I observed senior Washington officials – from several parts of the US executive branch, cruise through Myanmar. They would meet with Aung San Suu Kyi, have photos taken at the pagodas, and then breezed off in a matter of three or at most five days. Meanwhile most of the people of Myanmar continue to live much as they have for the last three hundred years.

Yes, in 2016, there are many more cars, tall hotels and luxury apartments, and even twenty-four-hour grocery stores, but those are mostly for "others." In 2016, most of the people of Myanmar still held tightly to the longyi and to their centuries old ways. But alas, *still* everything changes. When you travel to Myanmar, I recommend going slow. Take a walk along the back streets in Yangon with a Myanmar friend. Sit quietly in an out of the way tea shop in Mandalay and watch the beautiful dance of Myanmar life. It will be there waiting for you.

In mid-July 2016, just six months into its new fledgling democracy, Aung San Suu Kyi's government was facing a barrage of criticism. Critics in Myanmar and across the world were demanding change. Many wanted the new government to have moved much more quickly with the difficult issues of human rights and rebuilding the nation's schools and infrastructure.

Just six months after the historic election, one Myanmar businessman, quoted in the Myanmar Times, said, "I am really disappointed in her, I had hoped to see more interaction with the public and more economic progress." Change is coming to Myanmar, but one does not rebuild from fifty-five years of poverty and destruction in one-hundred days. When you arrive in Myanmar in 2018 or 2025, I fully expect you to find – for better or for worse – people living much as they did in 1948. Those people, I fully except, will still hold hope. For the Myanmar people, really for all of us, hope makes our present struggles less difficult. Believing in change and in a better tomorrow has sustained the happy-go-lucky people of Myanmar for generations.

Reverse Culture Shock

I put my body through thirty-two hours of return flights back to my life in the United States. Travel is almost always hard for me, and I arrived in Houston exhausted and in a fog. Coming back to United States was, for me, a bit of a shock. I landed in Houston a different version of myself. I no longer shy away from strange things, or from unfamiliar foods, or from ways that are not intrinsic to my rural route upbringing and my own tribe. The first days and months back in the United States required a re-adjustment. Not only had my perception of myself changed but my home environment had also changed during my Fulbright. Texas did not at first seem all that familiar. Seeing Americans for the first time in a while and from a new perspective was strange and an interesting gift. A few examples will suffice here. First, coming from a culture where very few people will ever say no, to one in which rather abrupt and even uncivil confrontation is not uncommon, took some readjusting. The culture in Myanmar is to strive to avoid any negative or unpleasant social feelings. Many people in the Houston airport simply do not practice that cultural norm. I saw a petty argument between airlines employees and a passenger that would be strangely out of place in the Yangon airport.

Second, being hungry after many hours of travel, we stopped at a restaurant on the way out of Houston and I was reminded of how large American meal portions are. Every part of the meal is significantly larger, including the drink. Our plates, glasses, and even silverware are larger. The size of a meal in Myanmar – even in an expensive Western hotel – is typically one-third the size of a typical American meal. Probably, in part, as a direct result of meal size, the American population is obviously and starkly more overweight than the Myanmar population. Arriving in Houston it was immediately obvious that many Texans are overweight or obese.

Finally, after teaching in three different Myanmar institutions and learning so much about them and the students and faculty, it took some re-adjusting once I

was back on my home campus. In some ways, I don't
think I will ever "re-adjust" to my home campus. I
have come to see it and all of the people in it in a new
light. Not a bad light, but yet a different light. In the
Fulbright year, I spent time with administrators,
faculty, and students in over fifteen different
institutions in Southeast Asia. All of those
experiences gave a new perspective and put the
administrators, faculty, and most importantly, the
students of The University of Texas at Tyler in a new
light.

Travel – living abroad – is a magnificent gift. I
remain ever grateful. Travel frees the mind from the
constraints of the known. If the traveler allows it, the
experiences will reshape perspective and give the gift
of a lifetime of memories. But once home, and after
the readjustments, then what does one do? I will
remember and share. In quiet and meditative
moments, I will recall the sounds of the monsoon
rain, the smells of unknown spices and foods, and the
many wonderful students and fascinating people I
met. Alison and I will probably chat a little too long
with the Burmese person who works in our local
grocery store. We will ask her which tribe her people
are from. I will go to conferences and share my
research. I will write and read the stories of others, so
that I can remember Burma and share the perspective,
the beauty, the struggles I experienced, and most of
all, so that I can remember to focus on the pure
pleasure of the dance.

Teaching Barefoot in Burma at Yangon University (2016).
Photo credit Khin Sandar.

Young nun with alms bowl in Yangon (2016).
Photo credit: Robert Sterken

Acknowledgements

◊

Grateful I Am

There is an old Irish proverb that says, "it is in the shelter of each other that the we live." My journey to Burma was made possible by the support, shelter, and care of many people. I could not have spent a complete year learning, teaching, researching, and writing without their support. It simply would not have been possible. I made many friends in Myanmar too many to list here, but I want to thank a few specifically for their extraordinary support.

Mr. Htoo Htoo Wah, an English professor and administrator at Myanmar Institute of Theology (MIT) was most gracious and generous with his time, support, and wisdom. Htoo Htoo very ably served as our "entry buddy" and greatly eased the transition from culture shocked American to an at-home expat. Alison and I will always treasure Htoo Htoo's friendship and support. I also want to express my sincere gratitude to Ms. Ohnmar Lwin for her kindness. As the chair of the Social Sciences Department, Ms. Lwin made teaching the wonderful MIT students a joy and pleasure. She led me, Alison, and my daughter, on many excursions out into the rural countryside to meet people and experience local Myanmar life. She arranged many interviews with monks and served as my interpreter during those visits. Ms. Starry Tun (Naw Say Say Tun) also worked hard to share information about local politics and served as a very able interpreter during interviews with monks. Dr. Samuel Ling, President of MIT, was a gracious host and generous with his support.

Dr. Chaw Chaw Sein, Chair and Head, of the International Relations Department at Yangon University is a champion for her students, faculty, and the people of Myanmar. I am grateful to her for providing me with excellent research and teaching assistants and for the opportunity to teach Yangon University Honors and graduate students.

Mr. Myat Thu, the President of the Yangon School of Political Science gave me the extraordinary opportunity to teach his amazing students in the school he and other political prisoners founded. Myat Thu set up interviews for me with many inspiring monks. I will always be grateful for his generosity, time, and the many inspiring lessons he shared with me.

I taught remarkable students at the Yangon School of Political Science. Two students, Than Toe Aung and Khin Sandar, spent a great deal of time and effort sharing the culture, food, and politics of Myanmar. They both are fine scholars and leaders who will one day be important and influential leaders. I am grateful to them both.

The United States Embassy in Yangon is staffed by extraordinary professionals who make a person proud to be an American. Ms. Sarah Quinzio, US Public Affairs Officer, was extraordinarily supportive, professional, and patient. It is no easy task to deal with incoming Fulbright scholars. Ms. Quinzio organized all of the excellent opportunities all of the scholars enjoyed in Myanmar. I also want to thank Ms. Kristen F. Bauer, Deputy Chief of Mission at the U.S. Embassy, for her warm hospitality, support, and friendship. Meals at the DCM Bauer's US Embassy home were among the best I had in Myanmar. Working with DCM Bauer in public events was a pleasure. The US State Department is very fortunate to have such professionals.

My time in Burma was made possible by the generous arrangement of four remarkable administrators on my home campus of The University of Texas at Tyler. Drs. Marcus Stadelmann, Scott Marzilli, Martin Slann, and Ross Sherman each in his own way supported and made the Fulbright journey possible. I will always be grateful to each of these gentlemen for their support and friendship.

Having their father spend a year in Burma was a significant sacrifice for my three adult children. I missed many special events, celebrations, and needed their distant support. I want to thank them for their diligent daily efforts to reach out across the time zones and stay in close touch with me.

My brother, Michael Sterken, spent time each day reaching out to me and chatting to ease the isolation. I am ever grateful my brother.

My father-in-law, Dr. William R. Johnson, not only supported the Fulbright journey but took care of family and many details on the home front during my absence. Bill also carefully edited the pages of this book. All errors are mine alone.

It is not possible to thank my life partner enough for all of her love, help, and support for this year long journey. Alison knew that I had to go and that it would not be easy. She understood the wanderlust and the seeking. That understanding did not make the journey any less difficult for her. She made Myanmar home. Alison also took care of so very many life details at home in Texas, including my aging and ill mother and all of the home-front demands that are required of people in our stage of life. Her willingness to take on all of those details made it possible for me to focus on teaching and on the monks and politics in Myanmar. Alison also carefully and lovingly read the pages of this book, supported the writing even when I did not believe in it, and edited it with skill and care. It was because of Alison that I was able to make this journey.

Robert Sterken with Yangon University Honors students (2016).
Photo credit: Yangon University.

About the Author

◊

Robert Sterken is an Associate Professor of Political Science at the University of Texas at Tyler. Professor Sterken is a Senior Fulbright Scholar who has taught politics in many places around the world, most recently in Burma/Myanmar, Thailand, and Cambodia. He has been teaching and writing about politics and power for twenty plus years. Sterken is married to the love of his life, Alison Johnson Sterken, an avid runner, yogi, reader and writer, traveler and global soul who lives mostly in Tyler, Texas.

Alison and Robert Sterken Shwedagon Pagoda (2015).
Photo credit U Htoo Htoo Wah.

62748373R00123

Made in the USA
Charleston, SC
21 October 2016